ANOTHER LIFE

ANOTHER LIFE

On Memory, Language, Love,
and the Passage of Time

THEODOR KALLIFATIDES

Translated from the Swedish by Marlaine Delargy

OTHER PRESS / NEW YORK

Verse on page 125 from *The Persians* by Aeschylus, translated by Robert Potter.
Reprinted by permission.

Production editor: Yvonne E. Cárdenas
Text designer: Jennifer Daddio / Bookmark Design & Media Inc.
This book was set in Bulmer MT and Bodoni Old Face
by Alpha Design & Composition of Pittsfield NH.

1 3 5 7 9 10 8 6 4 2

Library of Congress Cataloging-in-Publication Data

Names: Kallifatides, Theodor, 1938- author. | Delargy, Marlaine, translator.
Title: Another life : on memory, language, love, and the passage of time / Theodor Kallifatides ; translated from the Swedish by Marlaine Delargy.
Other titles: Ännu ett liv. English
Description: New York : Other Press, [2018] | "Originally published in Swedish as Ännu ett liv in 2017 by Albert Bonniers Förlag, Stockholm"—ECIP galley
Identifiers: LCCN 2017058667 (print) | LCCN 2018006806 (ebook) | ISBN 9781590519462 (ebook) | ISBN 9781590519455
Subjects: LCSH: Kallifatides, Theodor, 1938- | Authors, Swedish—20th century—Biography.
Classification: LCC PT9876.21.A45 (ebook) | LCC PT9876.21.A45 A5613 2018 (print) | DDC 839.73/74 [B]—dc23
LC record available at https://lccn.loc.gov/2017058667

TO KARL OTTO BONNIER

Nothing is more precious than a friend.

—*Aristotle*

I

It was a difficult time. My latest novel had taken up all my strength. I was exhausted, and thinking of abandoning my writing: giving up on it, before it gave up on me.

I was already on overtime, having completed my seventy-seventh year. One evening in the Folkoperan bar, the subject came up when I was chatting with Björn Wiman, the culture editor of *Dagens Nyheter*. He put forward the view that nobody should write after the age of seventy-five.

"It's okay until seventy-five, but then something happens to them," he said. He meant writers.

Had this "something" happened to me now?

I made a couple of halfhearted attempts to work on a few ideas, but got nowhere. Partway through a sentence I would be overcome by a feeling of weariness, the words didn't taste right in my mouth. How to move on?

On one of those days I went and stood under the shower in my studio with all my clothes on and let myself get absolutely soaking wet. The idea was to try out Chekhov's advice on how to recover from a failure. That was what it felt like: not being able to write was a major failure, a huge failure, and the unassuming Anton had suggested that one should do what a wet dog does. Shake off the water.

It didn't work. Quite the reverse. I ended up trembling with cold, and the sorrow burrowed even deeper into my soul. I was not only a wet dog but also a frozen ex-writer.

I had lived for seventy-seven years. The time weighed heavier than the water. It wasn't possible to lift that weight from my shoulders. How was I going to be able to write again?

I had read an interview with Karin Johannisson, one of the finest essayists we have ever had. She was only seventy, but she said she wasn't going to write anymore, because she had neither the strength nor the desire to be eaten up by a new literary project to that extent.

It didn't bear thinking about.

Was it still possible for me to organize my days around a text? The narrative filled every waking and sleeping moment when I was working. My heroines were close to me, and my heroes, who lay beside them, had to put up with my scorn or loathing if they were cowardly or cruel.

My heroines aroused boundless curiosity and desire. They walked before me or arm in arm with me, they came toward me scowling or smiling, they sat opposite me with their legs crossed, or giggled behind my back.

I knew how they dressed, what they read, what they liked in a man or in a woman, when they fell in love, and when they opened their arms for the first time.

Sometimes I would fall in love with one of them, and jealousy took over. Intense interrogation, over and over again. What did you say to him and what did he say to you? Where have you been? You call that dancing? It looked more like foreplay to me! What are you thinking about? I called and you didn't answer. And so on and so on.

In the evenings, my wife would occasionally ask, "What did you do today?"

"I've been with another woman."

She would laugh, but it was true. I was with Elena from *With the Coolness of Her Lips* in Australia or with Timandra in Athens two thousand five hundred years ago or with someone else somewhere else.

That was how my days had passed ever since 1969, when my first novel was published. No writer's block, no interruptions to the flow. Every book was a bridge to the next. Almost like love affairs. But now it was 2015, and my strength was dwindling. Did I have the energy to summon up the dedication and commitment that had carried me all these years?

My greatest fear has always been that I might leave myself open to ridicule. Write something so dire that even the gulls flying over Strömmen would snigger. I was more afraid of writing badly than not writing at all. But would I know if it was bad? Or would I terrorize my wise publisher?

One can always rely on the critics, of course. I couldn't. I had been part of the literary game of Ludo for far too long to take it entirely seriously. The decision to write or not to write was too important to allow someone else to make it for me.

This was about my life.

Aksel Sandemose—who spelled his name with *ks* because he didn't want a cross in the middle of it—is a writer who has won my heart and my mind. He used to say that if an author can stop writing, then he should.

Sandemose had another piece of advice. One of his close friends was a painter who had lost his beloved wife and was bemoaning the fact that he could no longer paint.

"Every time I stand in front of my easel, I see her face," his friend said.

"Well, paint her face," Sandemose replied.

I didn't have a face to paint, just a dull feeling of anxiety in my heart, an inarticulacy in my brain as if it were wrapped in cotton wool, a kind of permanent hangover. I might be able to write about why I couldn't write, but it wasn't exactly a pressing need. It would be better to stop.

Could I stop? I wasn't sure. Not being able to write is one thing. Deciding to stop trying is something quite different. When I mentioned it to my family, they just laughed and reminded me that I said the same at the end of every book. A couple of friends reacted in the same way. "Typical addictive behavior," one of them said. "Every time you get clean you decide to stop, then you go straight back to your drug of choice."

Although sometimes it's just not possible to write. Even an author as gifted as Göran Tunström had to abandon a manuscript in the middle of his work, because he simply couldn't write another line. Or a major author like Vilhelm Moberg, who chose death rather than artistic impotence.

Georges Simenon used to write at top speed. A two-hundred-page novel took him a couple of weeks. His routine was very straightforward. He shut himself in a room, his secretary provided him with food, and Simenon didn't come out until the new book was finished.

One day he followed the usual pattern. He locked himself in, and his secretary stationed himself outside the door, waiting for the familiar sound of the typewriter. Several hours passed, and he heard nothing. Suddenly Simenon emerged, pale and haggard after the fruitless search for the first sentence.

"*Ça y est*," he said.

Which means, "That's it."

He had written more than four hundred books, but he couldn't produce one more word. From that day on, he didn't write anything else as long as he lived.

In other words, my own fear was not irrational; the more I wrote, the greater the risk that it would all come to an end. The probability of something happening increases as time goes on and it hasn't yet happened.

It wasn't coquettishness either. I wasn't expecting the whole of Sweden to fall to its knees and beg me to continue. I wouldn't be summoned to Babel to explain myself. Most people wouldn't even notice. Very few people are fortunate enough to attract attention because they have stopped writing. I was under no illusions. But I was terrified of the emptiness that would take over my life. A series of days and nights as indistinguishable from one another as the long walkways in the apartment blocks built as part of the Million Program.

And yet I couldn't write. Why? It wasn't illness, it wasn't personal problems or the social climate or anything else. The spring from which my writing came lay within me. If this spring dried up, there was something wrong with me. I couldn't blame anything else, even if I wasn't completely in tune with contemporary society. I could write an essay or a discussion book about that kind of thing, but I didn't want to.

Sailors talk about a following wind. That's what writing is like. You are carried along, the narrative chooses its own pathways, anything can happen from one sentence to the next.

I yearned for that feeling. It wouldn't come.

Two months passed. I traveled to my studio every day. Once I got there, I did nothing but listen to music and talk on the phone. Mostly I played chess with my computer, which I had named Karl Otto after the man who has been my publisher for more than forty years, my constant opponent. Occasionally I beat the computer and my happiness knew no bounds, at which point I would go and stand in front of the mirror to check if you could actually see that I was losing my mind.

I loved spending time in my studio in the Söder district of Stockholm. The thought of walking up Mamsell Josabeth's steps filled me with joy every morning. That was where the first white, yellow, and blue flowers of the spring appeared, on the slope behind the Norwegian Church. Leaving my room each evening gave me just as much pleasure. The beautiful streetlamps spread a soft honey-colored glow all the way along Stigbergsgatan. It always took me a while to tear myself away from that particular sight.

You could say that was where I got a taste of a past that wasn't mine. It was the Stockholm of the old days. The building that housed my workspace used to be a spice emporium. I sat and wrote surrounded by the aroma of another century.

I really loved that room. "Good morning," I said each day when I walked in. "Have you had a restful night? Do you have anything for me today?" It had always obliged, throughout the years.

The material we use is not only in our heads, but all around us; it is part of the walls and the furniture, in the aroma of the coffee, in the glow of the lamp. On a perfect day you can write about absolutely anything.

"Give me an ashtray and I'll give you a story!" boasted the modest Chekhov. There are other days when you can't write about anything at all. I often arrived feeling peevish and miserable, only to find the writer within me ten minutes later. "My slave," as a colleague put it.

Why was that the case? I have no idea. Perhaps it was the previous tenant's aura that lived on. I had never met him, I had no idea what kind of person he was, apart from the fact that he presumably lived a lonely life, because he left behind a very narrow—narrower than normal—iron bed, more reminiscent of the torture chamber than of rest and pleasure.

It was painful to look at that bed. It exuded such loneliness that my eyes filled with tears, and I was afraid I would end up the same way. Alone in a very narrow iron bed. I sent it to a secondhand store, then I went to IKEA and bought a simple but comfortable bed that was neither single nor double but somewhere in between. It was called the Sultan. Marvelous.

That was where I had my siesta. My Swedish friends took a walk after lunch, except for Ernst. He ran instead. I couldn't do it. I felt sleepy as soon as I'd eaten. It was impossible to remain upright. I just had to lie down on my Sultan, and that was what I did.

The fact that I was secure in the knowledge of the sight that awaited me when I opened my eyes filled me with calm. Through one window I could see the dome of Katarina Church, and through the other Stockholm's harbor area, where large and small ships docked, carrying retirees and couples from all over the world.

My room was in a wooden building dating from the 1870s. It hadn't been restored since those days, apart from the décor. On one occasion an electrician had to dig out a channel for a cable. He fought like a demon.

"Jeez, it's harder than stone!" he said. He grabbed the piece of wood he had cut out and held it up to my big Greek nose.

"It still smells of pine," he said.

I had had so many wonderful years in my studio, and now I was going to live without it. The last few months had a nightmarish quality. I did everything the same as always: I arrived on time, made coffee, switched on the computer, but that was the end of it. I tried out various ideas: translating the *Iliad*, penning an essay on Aristotle's *Nicomachean Ethics*, writing a love story. They all died due to a lack of oxygen.

I had a problem. Not only with myself but also with society. It was agonizing to see Sweden changing, step by step. Social justice and solidarity were giving way to the visible and invisible power of the market. Education was becoming increasingly privatized, as was care. Teachers and doctors were turning into entrepreneurs, students and patients were becoming clients. It was all happening so fast that it didn't even have time to register as history. The pay gap was growing year by year. Greed was in the driver's seat, the boundless freedom of the individual was now the guiding star.

I couldn't adjust, and I was getting older in a world that felt more and more alien to me. In the end I didn't even dare to open my mouth. My objection was a given. I had gotten old and grumpy. A *gnällspik*, no less, to use a word that I love. A bellyacher.

Gnällspik! A fantastic invention.

And they say Swedish is a poor language.

My wooden house represented all the values that were slipping away. It was built with these values. The wood still smelled of wood after almost two hundred years, while even candles smelled bad these days. I usually lit one or two on gloomy winter afternoons. Thirty years ago when I started this habit, they spread a soft scent all around. Now I couldn't bear the acrid odor they gave off.

Am I exaggerating? A little, perhaps, but only a little.

The whole area was being transformed with bewildering speed. Stigberget was being excavated in order to provide underground parking beneath our feet. We protested, we wrote letters and signed petitions, but we were ignored, not only by the building contractors but also by the city of Stockholm and its functionaries. The city was experiencing the worst housing crisis in modern times, and they were building parking lots.

An unexpected consequence of the subterranean construction was that the rats went crazy and rushed out onto the streets waving red flags. They followed me when I was on my way to have lunch at Jimmy's, yet another Greek in the diaspora. The streets stank, people pissed all over the place, the cost of finding somewhere to live was going through the roof, and they were building parking lots.

That's what had happened in Stockholm, where spitting in the street was once regarded as a minor offense.

Fortunately there were also changes for the better—outdoor florists, for example. They put up their stalls every morning in a square or at an intersection and set out their flowers and plants, both in summer and in winter. The scent that rose up transformed their surroundings.

Down below my studio on Tjärhovsplan was Samira from Chile. She was energetic, knowledgeable, and cheerful. We always exchanged a few words in the morning, and in the evening if she was still there. Sometimes she would give me a flower to put on my desk. She had read one of my stories, but otherwise it was her daughter who read my books.

Occasionally I would linger for a while. I actually have a secret. I like to watch women buying flowers. They have a kind of glow about them. As far as men are concerned, it's all doom and gloom. They look as if they're about to purchase hand grenades.

Samira had set up her business all by herself, and she now employed three assistants. Somehow just seeing her put me in a good mood and made me want to get down to work. How hard can it be to write a book, when a single woman, a refugee from Chile, can start up and run a business with three employees?

The Greek, on the other hand, had erected his stall on Medborgarplatsen when he lost his job with Saab, which was going downhill fast. His progress too was astonishing. After a year or so he had five employees and he became a warmhearted philanthropist, taking care of the homeless, giving them food, and inviting them inside out of the cold. He also gave money to all the Roma begging in his area.

He worked inhumanly hard. He got up at four in the morning to go to the market in Västberga even though his wife tried to pull him back into bed. That was their time; if they didn't make love then, it wouldn't happen. He didn't get home until nine o'clock in the evening.

"After we've eaten, we switch on the TV to watch the news. I haven't seen the end of *Aktuellt* for years. I fall asleep in my armchair. Fortunately Christina wakes me up, makes me brush my teeth as if I were a three-year-old, then I collapse into bed, half-dead. Who can play the energetic Greek lover under those circumstances?"

Every day, the same routine. First the flowers must be bought, then the stall must be erected and his wares displayed. Then it's a question of trying to sell as much as possible. It is important to recognize the customers, chat with them, in certain cases even flirt a little with them. At the end of the day everything must be packed away, the takings counted and deposited in the bank's night box, and the following morning it starts all over again.

"You've become like Sisyphus," I said.

He'd never heard of Sisyphus, so I told him the myth. Zeus had punished Sisyphus by making him push a boulder up a hill, but when he reached the top, the boulder rolled back down again, and Sisyphus had to start over from the beginning.

My tale had consequences.

One morning the Greek looked different. He hadn't shaved, and he didn't smile when he saw me.

"What's wrong? Has Christina closed the pearly gates to paradise?"

He shook his head.

"Would you like a cup of coffee?"

We went to the café on Medborgarplatsen and he told me the whole story. He had decided he wasn't going to fall victim to the same fate as Sisyphus. He didn't remain at his post, but instead left his stall in the hands of his employees and went for a walk. It was one of those glorious sunny winter days. First he went to Fatbur Park to enjoy the sight of the young moms playing with their children. However, most of them had brought a dog along, and there was a cacophony of barking dogs, screaming kids, and the moms' cell phones ringing nonstop.

He didn't last long. Fifteen minutes, maybe. Then he went for an espresso in an Italian café, where the owner had only one thing on his mind: Juventus. There was no point in trying to talk to him about anything else, but his coffee was good. My poor friend moved on to the Pakistani restaurant, but he couldn't stand the smell of curry. He finally opted for a Danish hot dog from the other Greek on Medborgarplatsen, who looked worried as he asked, "Do you trust your employees? They'll steal the shirt off your back!" But our hero was determined not to suffer the same fate as Sisyphus, so he set off for Katarina churchyard.

He sat on a bench and counted all the passersby, who would be dead one day. It wasn't easy to grasp the fact that all these people were going to die. He sank deeper and deeper into his thoughts, until he started talking to himself. "Won't any of them survive?" he asked, getting angry.

He realized he was approaching a critical point. Sitting on a bench in the middle of the day talking to himself just wasn't acceptable. He hurried back to his flower stall and immediately began to banter with his staff. It was an absolute joy.

"Listen to me, my friend. You may be an author and a philosopher, but you haven't understood the myth of Sisyphus. Zeus wasn't punishing him. Quite the reverse. He was taking pity on him. Man is nothing without his work."

I had never heard this interpretation. You learn a lot in a foreign country. He was right. Now that I had left my studio, it was obvious.

"Man without his work is *haram*," he had stated firmly, using the Turkish word that had been adopted by the Greek language. Life without work is a waste. That was the terrible conclusion he had reached.

It sounded like an exaggeration, and yet the same applied to me. It was in my studio that I functioned best, and the days were filled to the brim with significance.

That was where everything had a role to play, even if I didn't always realize it. The wood-burning stove, for example, which I didn't use but liked to look at. How carefully, how meticulously it was constructed. And then there was the maker's name, Bolinder, etched in beautiful ornate lettering. The industry was gone, but the old premises were being converted into luxury offices and apartments.

Through my window I could see the golden bell tower of Katarina Church, shining like a little sun on bright afternoons. And the bells that rang and sent me into a dreamlike state could have been the church bells in my Greek village, or my local church in Athens. There were heavenly pathways stretching between my two countries. The rambling rose outside my window kept on flowering late into the fall, as if it were embracing the summer that had gone.

In the end it didn't matter why I was so contented in that room, only the fact that I felt that way. I made my coffee, lit my pipe, switched on the computer, and the world came pouring in. That was how my life had been for forty years, sometimes in other rooms too, in other areas, in other cities, on trains and in hotels, overseas and here at home. I worked all the time. That was my life. That was my soul. I brought it out in my writing every day.

How could I deny it?

One afternoon I happened to walk past a school, Södra Latin. The children had just finished and were on their way home, but a small group was blocking my path. A girl, presumably the most daring of them all, boldly asked me, "What's your name?"

I hesitated for a second, but only a second.

"Theodor."

I thought she would snigger. I thought wrong. The young, challenging gaze softened.

"That's a lovely name," she said, inclining her head elegantly.

It was on that very afternoon that my decision was made. I ought to change my life in the same matter-of-fact way as I had given my name to those children. Rediscover what I had lost.

I left my studio, sold everything that could be sold, gave away everything that could be given away, threw out everything that ought to be thrown out, and closed the door behind me.

"Goodbye, my friend," I said.

I had no idea what the consequences would be.

At first it was a relief. No need to rush around in the mornings, no need to wonder what clothes to wear—for example, would I need my long johns?—no need to hurry to the station in order to avoid missing the train, which was usually late anyway, and the greatest relief of all, escaping my pounding heart—would I be able to write something today? It was my pounding heart that prevented me from falling asleep even when I was bone-weary.

I was worried about missing something. It felt like dropping off to sleep when you were on watch in the military, the only time when an ordinary soldier had real responsibility and a little power. Not even the commander could get by without the correct password. I liked being on guard duty, watching over my sleeping comrades.

It was the same with my writing. I was keeping watch. If I woke at three in the morning, I would get up, make some coffee, light my pipe, and write at the kitchen table until it was time to catch the train to my "wolf's lair."

Why did writing carry such weight in my life? What did it give to me? What did it replace? I think it was like being on guard duty in the military. I wrote without asking for permission and without anyone being able to forbid me from doing it. Perhaps that was exactly what it was: I was taking responsibility for my world.

Now it was time to leave all this behind. It was time to emigrate from myself, just as I had emigrated from my country.

During those first few days of not working, I hardly wanted to get out of bed. Fortunately we—my wife and I—have separate rooms. Her name is Gunilla, but my dear father couldn't pronounce *u* and always called her Giounilla. Presumably because he had learned Turkish when he was a child, where the diphthong *iou* is very common.

I thought about him a great deal. He hadn't retired until the age of eighty-two, when no one was prepared to offer him a job any longer.

Why was I considering a withdrawal? Clearly I had hit some kind of crisis. I wasn't the only one. Most writers end up there at some point. Why didn't I keep trying? My publisher tempted me with very generous advances in an attempt to get me to carry on. My books were selling well, if not quite so well as in the past.

What was it that drove me to give up?

I was tired, no doubt about it. And yet I functioned as a writer in my daily life, regarding it as material for future projects. Significant details were noted, things that might be of use were saved on the hard drive of my brain, whether it was a face I had seen for ten seconds or the memory of a garden with almond trees in blossom outside my village seventy years ago.

Life was still arousing, albeit not as erotic as in the past, when I would see the sea and want to make love to it. Now I no longer saw it, but rather remembered it.

Was it time to go back to my roots? Could it be that what remained was not the future but the past?

This was the kind of thing that occupied my mind.

I have to admit it: I was also ashamed. Poverty in Stockholm was becoming more and more evident. Beggars on the streets, in the squares, on the commuter trains. The homeless. At the same time, hatred toward foreigners was growing, asylum seekers' centers were being set on fire, support for the most virulently anti-immigration party was increasing with every new poll.

I wasn't just an immigrant, I was also a Greek. This wasn't Greece's finest hour. Its national debt had reached astronomical levels. The whole of Europe was burning with indignation at these idle Greeks who were born pensioners. A political cartoon in a Dutch newspaper showed a fat Greek in pajamas with a bold expression on his face, holding out both hands to the EU. With one hand he was begging for the European taxpayers' money, and with the other he was giving them the finger.

It reminded me of Dr. Goebbels's posters during the German Occupation, which depicted the Greeks as brazen apes chasing German virgins. It also made me think of the foreword to my novel *Masters and Peasants*, in which I declared that I wanted to talk about my country without shame and without pride. The year was 1973.

In 2015 I needed all the pride I could summon up in order to cope with the shame that overwhelmed me. Greece was being humiliated every single day, by everyone.

The EU worked out what Greece owed, while at the same time, on a daily basis thousands of refugees risked and sometimes lost their lives in the Aegean archipelago. I had seen them for myself in the spring on the island of Symi, where I had gone to see the two very beautiful monasteries. Most of the refugees were young men, but there were also women and children. It was the middle of the day, and the heat was tiring. The newly arrived refugees lay exhausted in the square outside the dock office. They didn't speak to one another, they didn't attempt to speak to anyone else either. There was complete silence. They had given themselves up to their fate, which at that moment consisted of the two young dock guards.

I sat down in a modest café on the narrow shoreline. Thirty seconds later a beautiful woman appeared in front of me. She was tall, fair-haired, slender. She must be a tourist wanting to ask me something, I thought. In fact, she was the owner of the café. I ordered a double espresso, because I know that a single espresso in the tourist spots in Greece is regarded as a half espresso.

"What will become of these people?" I wondered.

"Things will work out for them just as they did for us," she replied.

There weren't many people in the café, so she told me her story. She had come to Greece from Albania in her mother's arms. It was hard at first. Then her parents found work, she went to school, learned the language with lightning speed, and at the age of seventeen she met her husband, who was from Symi. And now...

"Now I have two grandchildren."

Her voice was full of defiant confidence.

I couldn't help myself: "Why didn't I have a grand-mother like you!"

Thanks to this compliment, I wasn't allowed to pay for my coffee.

I shared her view. Things work out. My father was a refugee and I was an emigrant. We had both made it.

Times were different now.

I could see it when I traveled to Athens two months later. In my part of town, the cafés were full of the unem-ployed. The number of street hawkers was growing by the day. I bought ten lighters from one of them. Not a single one worked.

The entrance to a major clothing store in the city center was guarded by two large German shepherds, which had been trained to distinguish between different types of people. They wagged their tails when a genuine customer appeared but growled threateningly at poor immigrants and Greeks, men and women alike.

"For God's sake," exclaimed an elderly woman, "we didn't have dogs outside the shops even during the Occupation!"

(That's what the time between 1940 and 1944 is called. Four years of the Nazi terror regime and shortages of everything.)

Poverty isn't only visible; you can smell it. An acrid odor mingled with expensive perfumes had settled over the city center. "The stench of humanity," my friend Kostakis would say, if he were still alive.

Beggars everywhere. Some were crippled, showing their wounds. Women lying on the street with small children in their arms. Stylish young men, pleading on their knees. And we walked past, some of us ashamed and embarrassed, some with studied indifference.

THE DRACHMA IS THE OLDEST COIN IN THE WORLD, a sign outside the Greek National Bank informed us. But the drachma no longer existed. However, it was possible to see the remains of ancient Athens beneath the foundations of the bank.

It can't be helped. I am struck by a low-intensity dizziness when faced with such contemporary experiences. Fantasy images of the daily lives of the ancient Athenians are mixed up in my head with the reality around me. Everything is overlaid by poverty, utter destitution, the homeless, all those who don't have a roof over their head.

My brain is split in two like a ripe watermelon, while my heart shrivels like a snail. That's what makes me dizzy.

Exarcheia Square is a place I always go to whenever I am in Athens. That's where my old high school was during the 1950s, and where I would sometimes sit with my girlfriend, in spite of draconian restrictions. We would eat honey mixed with butter. When I couldn't afford to pay, we simply sat on a bench beneath the acacia tree.

Now the square was occupied by drug dealers and their clients. Young girls who were prepared to sell themselves for the next hit. The dealers strolled around with their wares in a body belt, sometimes a fight broke out. Not a police officer in sight.

A dealer suddenly started furiously beating a skinny little girl. She didn't even dare to scream with pain. Nobody intervened apart from her boyfriend, who summoned up the remnants of his human dignity and stepped in.

"You'd hit a woman, would you, you bastard?" he yelled. The dealer punched him in the chest and he went down.

I didn't get a wink of sleep that night. It was impossible to forget the boyfriend's voice. It was hoarse, under the influence, without hope, yet still human. He hadn't given up.

"You'd hit a woman, would you, you bastard?"

At three o'clock in the morning, I went out onto the balcony of my hotel room. In the distance, the dark mass of the mountains, the sparsely lit communities on the hills surrounding the city. The Acropolis glowed in the night like an incomparably large butterfly.

I wanted to shout as loudly as I could so that everyone would hear me.

"You'd hit Greece, would you, you bastards?"

I didn't do it.

Never before had I seen my city in that way. Poverty was an old friend, but not this misery. Boarded-up shops, unlit streets, the homeless sleeping everywhere, the stench of excrement, and on top of all this, an air of violence that made my heart beat faster. For the first time I could remember, I was afraid to go out alone in Athens.

That was the most humiliating aspect. The ultimate alienation. People gave me good advice. Don't go there, don't carry too much money, don't carry too little money, because then they might get mad and beat you up.

Who were "they"? Some of the perpetrators were certainly Greeks, but my would-be advisers were referring not to them but to the immigrants, the refugees. The collective gaze saw only the collective guilt. I had felt it too, in Sweden, when the crisis surrounding the Greek national debt began. After fifty-one years of life in Sweden, I became a Greek again, shuttling from one radio station to the next, from one TV channel to another. I had my part in the national guilt of the Greeks.

One evening in the square in my part of Athens, I sat down at one of the simple cafés offering "whores' food," as my mother used to call it—grilled chicken or pork or something else that is quick and easy. The waiter was from Albania, but his Greek was very good.

"Feta, chorta [cooked dandelion greens], and retsina as usual?" he asked with a smile.

I had eaten there just once before, yet he remembered not only me but also my ascetic order. It made me want to give him a hug.

He was no more intelligent than the other waiters, his memory was no better. But he possessed the alertness of the foreigner.

He saw, heard, learned, and remembered with all of his senses. There was no rest, and at night he slept as lightly as a hare. I had been there, and I knew. People don't sit down and wait for death.

If Europe showed a little more goodwill, things would work out for all the refugees. But Europe wanted its money.

II

On the first day without my studio and without my work, I rejoiced in the thought that I would be able to sleep as late as I wanted. However, I woke at half past three, and the morning star was shining so brightly, as if it were calling me in for questioning, and I had nothing to say in my defense.

I went back to bed. Strangely enough, I fell asleep once more. Two hours later it was time to get up. It was wonderful to think that I would be able to read my newspaper without constantly glancing at the clock, but I hadn't realized that I would be sharing it with my wife. As long as I was working, there was no problem. She was still in bed when I bent down and gave her a kiss before I set off. "Mm," she would say, without waking up.

Now she didn't say "mm" but prepared her breakfast with extraordinary care. It was by no means as simple an affair as mine: two slices of bread that I baked myself each Saturday, one with a little cheap Abba fish roe and the other with cheese and plum jelly, which I also made myself every summer on the island of Gotland. Naturally, I ate with the morning paper spread out in front of me, like a map to help me prepare for the day's activities.

I loved those mornings. So did my wife. But now we were both in the kitchen at the same time. She was wearing her red robe—the blue one that I thought suited her better was in the wash. She kissed the back of my neck and began the breakfast ceremony.

First she broke an egg, and let out an exclamation of surprise. The egg—in spite of the fact that it was unusually small—had a double yolk. We normally bought eggs on Gotland from a nearby farm, simply taking as many as we wanted and placing the money in a box. We hardly ever saw anyone.

We admired the double yolk for a while before it joined two strips of bacon in the frying pan. Then she cut a few slices of a red pepper, one slice of cheese, and a very thin piece of bread, which she placed on a plate next to the hob.

My father was also fond of very thin slices of bread, and my mother, who took great pleasure in her food, used to tease him. I also teased my wife, because I liked to cut my bread very thick, but she ignored me and began to line up all her vitamins, a number of capsules that were supposed to strengthen her joints. Then she switched on the radio while boiling two gallons of water for her tea.

This made me think about my friend Odysseas, who was in the habit of taking everything to the extreme. He stayed in my studio for a while with the aim of getting away from Greek food, because he wanted to lose some weight. For a whole month he followed a regime that he claimed had been invented by the Israeli army. He ate nothing but cucumber. However, one day he just couldn't cope anymore. I caught him red-handed, eating an entire gâteau all by himself hidden behind the bushes on Mariatorget.

In the evenings we played simple card games that required only luck. He kept on beating me, and boasted, "Good heavens, what a player I am!"

I said nothing, because what was there to say?

One Sunday Odysseas came to our house. He wanted to cook dinner for us in order to show off his skills. My wife was perfectly happy with the arrangement; they were both loud and loved their food. They clattered forks and spoons against plates and glasses, stirred the contents of various pans with passion and intensity, and fell on the food when it was ready.

"Slow down!" I said to Gunilla.

Odysseas sprang to her defense. "Let the girl enjoy her food, you sadist."

He too had been gone for a while. My dead companions were increasing in number.

As far as my wife was concerned, one thing was certain: I would go first. She is exactly five years and five days younger than me, and much healthier. Seeing her eat made me happy. She had a way of tilting her head to the right—a habit left over from the time when she had long hair—and opening her mouth a fraction earlier than necessary before pushing in the food with an almost sardonic smile on her lips, as if she were saying, "Just you wait."

She took half the newspaper as well.

We had been married for forty-six years, but we weren't a symbiotic couple. We didn't dream of doing everything together, or at the same time. We both wanted to be independent, and we were. As long as we were working, it wasn't a problem, nor when Gunilla retired at the age of sixty. I carried on going off to work every morning, and she could have her day exactly as she wished. For seventeen years she had had the entire house and the morning paper to herself.

Now we were both at home. She was uncomfortable, walking back and forth in the kitchen without looking at me. I felt equally ill at ease. By now I should be sitting at my computer, I should be working.

Suddenly her cell phone rang. It wasn't even nine o'clock. Who the hell was calling her at this hour? Had this been going on all along, with the phone ringing as soon as I'd left the house? However, I didn't say anything; I merely signaled to her that she could take the call in the living room.

Meanwhile my mind continued to work overtime. She must have been seeing someone else during all those years of running around in forests and on the shore with other lively individuals who had taken early retirement.

Not to mention all those meetings, evenings at the theater and the opera, women's groups. In my youth I had been a real Othello. I had once seen my girlfriend in Athens smile at another man, and I had fainted with the pain.

That was all over. These days I didn't even have the energy to faint. One good thing about growing old is that you think more about the future of others than your own. Gunilla was still attractive even though she had turned seventy. That made me happy. It is one of life's great mysteries that you can like the same face for forty-six years.

At the same time, I felt as if I was intruding on her private life like an uninvited guest. Fortunately, as I said before, we each had our own room. But I went to my room only to sleep. I didn't read, write, or smoke in there. I did all of those things in my studio in town. That was where I kept my books, my records, my pipes. My room at home felt alien, joyless and cramped.

Was I really going to spend my days in this prison?

Pain pierced my heart.

What had I done? It was sheer idiocy to leave my nest.

What was it I missed? Above all my morning walk of about a mile from home to the train station, even if it was sometimes a pain—particularly in the winter. My legs had gotten used to it. As had my soul. I would join up with a neighbor, exchange a few words with a dog owner, especially the very pleasant former bank manager who was out with his little dachshund. She was curious about everything and kept on stopping and sniffing at the ground. "She's reading the morning paper," the bank manager said cheerfully. I also met children on their way to school. Some of them saw me as a familiar uncle; they would say hello and we would chat for a while. Two sisters called me "Luther," according to their mother, who laughed as she told me without explaining the reason behind this nickname. Presumably it was because the girls saw me heading off to work at the same time every morning with my rucksack on my back, and the Swedes talk of "carrying Luther on your back."

I kept myself informed about what was going on in the area. Who had bought the latest Volvo model, who was away on vacation, who was replacing the roof, who was thinking of selling their house, and sometimes even the reason why. Divorce and old age were the most common triggers.

I followed the seasons in the gardens. Spring, summer, fall, and winter. Apple, cherry, and pear blossom. Lilac and bird cherry. The scent of the flowers, the smell of fruit that had fallen from the trees. The changing light. One spring afternoon in 1968 I had walked along this same route with no idea that my life was about to take a different turn.

The girl who became my wife was waiting for me at the gate of her family home. I was to meet her parents. A few years later we built our house on the plot next door.

That was the kind of thing that drifted through my mind on the way to the station. Sometimes, during periods of intense work, I took a different route to avoid everyone and everything.

From Södra station, where I got off the train, I had another walk of just over a mile to my studio. Each day I met the same people. We recognized one another without knowing anything about one another. We exchanged a brief smile, like an affirmation of our pleasure at the fact that we were still alive, and went on our way.

In the city, simply switching sidewalks was enough to step into a new adventure. There were days, especially in the early spring, when I didn't want to go straight to work. I would head for the graveyard at Katarina Church instead. Among many others, there lay a man I knew and liked: Johan Bergenstråhle. He had made the film of my novel *Foreigners*. We wrote the script together, while one of the liveliest, most imaginative and multitalented individuals I have ever met wandered around the apartment with a glass of wine mixed with water, one ass cheek bare because she had cut a big hole in her jeans. That was Marie-Louise Ekman.

Johan had died suddenly and relatively young.

I liked to sit in the graveyard, a little intoxicated by the spring and by death and by all those diffuse feelings and thoughts, utterly convinced that everything had a meaning even though I was unable to write it down.

By the time I reached my studio, I was already sated with life. I don't know how else to express it. I needed nothing more. Or whatever I might need, I could find it in my writing.

Those were my thoughts as I sat down at the computer in my room at home. I couldn't settle. I had ants in my pants, as they say. Instead of writing, I picked up an old Gotland newspaper and came across a couple of words I hadn't seen before: *ostor*—unbig!—and *fingå*—to go for a fine walk. A wave of happiness swept over me. Some words are irresistible. You have to taste them right away.

"I'm going out for a fine walk in this unbig sun," I called out to my wife. She was absorbed in her emails and didn't hear me.

Out in the street I wasn't sure what to do. Where should I go now that I didn't have to catch the train? Should I wander around aimlessly? And if I wasn't writing anymore, what should I think about?

I strolled along for a while with an empty mind, but I was soon joined by my friend Kostas. He used to be my shield, and now he was dead.

He was the one who protected me when we demonstrated against the junta in Greece, in both Sweden and Iceland, where the police officers were tall, strong, and ready for a fight. He took many a blow, but I didn't.

Kostas, who used to be a builder's laborer and had a back like a barn door, always positioned himself in front of me, like a wall. He was always ahead of me, always first.

He left in the same way. First. A serious illness took its toll on him and he refused to tolerate it. Death would not humiliate him. I imagine he died alone in his sickroom at three o'clock in the morning. We remained behind to remember him.

By now I had strayed far from my local area and had ended up in a place that had been a small village a hundred years or so ago. There were a few buildings left from those days, and plenty of new houses with expensive cars parked outside. There was also a ruin; the council had put up a sign in front of it. These tumbledown walls had been the village school. However, it was not this information that moved me so much, but the fact that the path leading to the ruin had its own sign: THE OLD SCHOOL TRACK. It took my breath away for a moment.

I followed it through open fields and meadows until it disappeared into the forest like a frightened snake. This track had been created by children's footsteps. No one drove them to school back then. They had to get there under their own steam six times a week, on sunny or overcast days, in the rain and the wind and the cold. Week after week. Year after year. Back and forth.

These were the children who would one day trans-form Sweden from an almost feudal society into Social Democracy's modern welfare state.

Their track was still here.

What would those early Social Democrats say about the refugee crisis? I wondered. Society was divided. Some people wanted nothing to do with the refugees. Others thought that Sweden ought to uphold the rights of asylum seekers without reservation. I thought so too. But the stream of refugees kept on coming. One hundred and sixty thousand people sought asylum within a very short period. The authorities concerned couldn't cope, because their hands were tied by outdated rules and regulations aimed at making life easier for the officials rather than addressing the needs of the refugees. Panic wasn't far away. At that point the Social Democratic government decided to close the border, more or less. The move was described as unavoidable.

I didn't share this view, and I said so. Partly because human rights cannot be negotiable on a case-by-case basis, and partly because in the near future Sweden would need these people in order to maintain a healthy demographic balance and a functioning employment market.

My words did not fall on fertile ground.

I had already raised my head above the parapet on a previous occasion. After the terrible attack on the office of the satirical magazine *Charlie Hebdo* in Paris, a debate on the freedom of expression blew up. Sweden's traditions in this area are formidable. The prevailing view was that there should be no boundaries when it came to what a person could say, as long as there was no harassment of particular ethnic or religious groups.

Voltaire was quoted over and over again. "I disapprove of what you say, but I will defend to the death your right to say it." I don't know if Voltaire had said this before or after the cheese, but I'm sure he didn't mean it in the way in which it is often interpreted—namely, as the right to offend.

I was tormented. For a start, I don't believe that all statements are "opinions." For example, it is not an opinion if you say that all Greeks are lazy, or that Jews are subhuman. It is an exhortation to treat these people differently from others, and not just the people but also their faith, their beliefs, their system of values, their standards, their aesthetics, their way of life. It involves assuming the authority to attack these people's right to exist. That's how Nazism began. The Jews became sub-human, their existence was compromised to the point where there appeared to be no other solution but to eliminate them.

Boundless freedom of expression was also about both resources and power. If you were outside the mass media system, you had virtually no opportunity to express yourself.

It is one thing to comment on general matters and quite another to comment on your neighbors. All freedoms have a natural limit: the other person. Whatever you do, whatever you say must take into account the other person's existence. You can ignore this, of course, but there are consequences. Bitterness, hatred, and terrorism arise, even out-and-out war. And by that stage hiding behind Voltaire is of no help at all.

If we want to understand each other, we must first accept that the other person exists, and may have different principles. Only in equal relationships can there be genuine understanding, mutual obligations and rights. When I was a high school student in Athens, we read a famous account of a quarrel between the leaders of ancient Athens and Sparta. The latter became angry and raised his hand to deliver a blow, but the Athenian said calmly, "Strike me, but listen first!" That was what happened, and the Athenian won the argument.

It was time to listen to what the weak in society had to say.

No one stops being a Christian because Christ is mocked. No one stops being a Muslim because Muhammad is mocked. Quite the reverse, in fact. The Christians become more Christian, the Muslims more Muslim.

Almost everyone grasped these simple points, apart from a number of editors, journalists, and artists. They believed they were entitled to a freedom with no boundaries, they defended their sacred and exclusive right to despise, insult, and make fun of others and their beliefs. They behaved like drill sergeants toward people who were not under their command.

I became more and more infuriated by this arrogance.

It is said that only man can commit suicide. There is one exception: the scorpion. I have seen them with my own eyes in my Greek village. When they are caught in a grass fire, they search for a way out. When they realize there is no escape, they calm down and sting themselves to death before the fire reaches them.

Certain democratic freedoms resemble scorpions in that they can destroy themselves. It is possible to introduce tyranny or a dictatorship by democratic means. In a democratic election it is possible to vote in a party whose aim is to bring down democracy. It is possible to strangle freedom of expression with the help of freedom of expression. We have the freedom to put forward opinions aimed at totally or partly strangling the opinions of others.

This situation is not news to anyone. It is usually referred to as "the dilemma of democracy." The tragic events in Paris were largely interpreted as an attack on the freedom of expression and opinion.

Regardless of whether this view is correct—personally, I don't agree—it may be appropriate to discuss the extent of these freedoms. There could well be values that are greater, such as peace, dialogue between different cultures and people, or the equal value of people.

Freedom of opinion is a typical scorpion idea when it also allows the view that it should be forbidden. An individual or an organization has the right to express this, to hand out leaflets, to organize meetings, sometimes to give its opponents a bloody nose, at which point they can be condemned for the violence, but not for the opinion.

Society does not want to and cannot forbid opinions, but it does want to and can forbid actions, or so they say. A clear line is drawn between opinions and actions according to the traditional dualism and the difference between body and soul.

Opinions are somehow seen as having a presence which is not physical. In that way they are unreal. They occur within time and space without actually existing. Words are compressed air. There is nothing there to grab hold of.

If you move a chair in the dining room, you can see the change, even if no one mentions it. Something has happened. Actions, unlike opinions, have a physical reality.

I wonder if we're getting it wrong here.

My maternal grandmother was not a philosopher, and she used to say that "words have no bones, but they can break bones." She knew what we all know: a word can cause more pain, more damage than the sharpest knife. As far as she was concerned, saying something and doing something were exactly the same.

She wasn't a philosopher, she couldn't even write her name—her signature was a cross. She was small and sickly and had lost all her teeth before she reached the age of forty. She chewed on hard roots with her gums so that I could manage them when I was three years old and there was nothing else to eat. That was in 1941, and it wasn't grasshoppers that consumed everything but an occupying army.

My grandmother lived through two world wars, several Balkan wars, and one civil war. When my father was taken away by the Nazis and we didn't know where he was, my grandmother set off to look for him. Her provisions were a chunk of bread, some olives, and an onion. She found him in a prison far away from home. The guards refused to let her visit him, but she stood at the gate and said that she was going nowhere until she had seen her daughter's husband. In the end they gave in.

When people asked her how she had coped with all that, she didn't answer with words. She pointed to the sky. She had faith. The icons in the village church were not valuable, but she would have defended them with her life. At home she had a miniature chapel where she kept her bridal crown and an icon of the Virgin Mary.

How stupid would you have to be to claim the right to desecrate her icons, to spit on her bridal crown, on her faith, to denigrate her life and refer to such barbarism as democratic freedom? And as if that weren't enough, to insist that you're not *doing* anything.

My grandmother wasn't tall, but as far as moral height was concerned, she was unsurpassed. I wish I had a tenth of her stature.

Opinions are actions or provoke actions, and not all statements are opinions. We ought to be able to support an opinion with logical and moral arguments, while taking into account known facts.

In the leaflets distributed by the German occupying force in Athens 1941–1945, the Greeks were depicted as apes up in the trees. I have seen these leaflets, both as a child and an adult, and I was seized by rage and despair. I probably wouldn't shoot dead the person who produced this propaganda, but I couldn't regard it as art, or as an example of the Gestapo's freedom of expression. I still can't.

I felt sick when it became fashionable in Greece to draw cartoons of Angela Merkel with a Hitler mustache. That's not satire. That's war.

In Sweden we have been spared the worst for quite a long time. We are more or less entirely secularized; we have left a guilty conscience, shame, and honor behind us. The barbarians can concern themselves with that kind of thing. No one can get at us. No one can insult or offend us.

Large parts of the world haven't gotten that far. We can hold the view that they ought to have progressed, but we can't force them. Opinions are not only actions but often lethal weapons. In all known wars, the opposing sides attack each other's beliefs and symbols. There has to be a limit to how naïve we can allow ourselves to be. If democratic freedoms are to have a meaning, they must be based not on themselves but on another overarching standard. A culture, a civilization is judged equally on the freedoms it embraces and those it eschews.

Everything that is not forbidden is not necessarily permissible.

The standard that should carry the greatest importance for both the state and the individual is the equal value of all human beings. Every other principle should stem from this.

I wrote an article about this subject, and there was something of a storm. How could it be that an author— me—was not prepared to defend Freedom of Expression? I was summoned all over the place to explain myself. I didn't oblige. I had lost the will to do so.

I had also lost respect for these matadors of the new liberalism. I had expected more generosity toward the weak, more empathy.

I was wrong.

The world had taken a new direction. The new capitalism was winning on a broad front. Globalization, which in fact simply meant that capital could do whatever it wanted, became the guiding star.

I spoke to young people, and most of them were tired of society's focus on possessions, on the hunt for fresh pleasures, on the lack of ideology. They were searching, but without finding what they were looking for. The traditional left had lost its former luster. The Green Party showed clear signs of having lost its way, and the Social Democrats were offering only the same old thing. This left nothing but extreme movements to the right of everything, or militant Muslims. Young men and women, some born and raised in Sweden, turned to ISIS.

My generation of Greeks left our country in order to escape poverty. Young Swedes were leaving one of Europe's wealthiest and definitely most modern countries in order to...what? Presumably they didn't recognize the ancient and the free, as the national anthem says. Sweden had become a marketplace where everything was for sale, but not to everyone.

They were wrong, but that was how they felt.

What was it Sartre had said? Either you die for something, or you die for nothing. The volunteers from Sweden preferred to die for something.

Once upon a time long ago I had written that man needs a meaning in life, not so much in order to live but to be able to die. It may be that it is honorable to die for what you believe in, but not to kill others for those beliefs.

Life both ends and continues, not in heaven or the Islands of the Blessed, but in the consequences of our actions.

That was the kind of thing that went through my mind on those long walks, waiting for the evening, which was always a pleasant time. Gunilla and I chatted over dinner about our children and grandchildren, about the world in general, whether there was anything worth watching on TV—the answer was usually no if you weren't a fan of crime series.

Gunilla would settle down at her computer while I went out onto the balcony to smoke my pipe. I ought to give up smoking. My lungs have taken a hammering. But still I carried on, if not to the same extent as in the past. My pipe and I had been married for fifty-five years, and now I was trying to change it from wife to mistress. It was working—kind of. But not in the evenings after dinner.

I made my way to the balcony, where I paraphrased Horace's poetry to myself. "You do not know how many winters Zeus has given you. This could be the last."

Of course I couldn't hear the waves of the Tyrrhenian Sea, as in Horace's poem, but I could see the lights of my neighbors' houses, the trembling leaves of the aspens, the fir tree trying to grow taller than every other tree around it, and I talked to myself, quietly and calmly.

What does it matter if you die tonight? You have seen these lights and these trees for many years. Even when you are dead, you will remember them. Life is not a dream, merely a shadow between time and light. Death robs you of nothing. You have tasted all pleasures. You have seen your woman give birth to your children. You have seen your son become a man and your daughter become a woman. You have seen the cherry tree grow, the waves of the sea polish the pebbles, the snakes intertwine. What more does this world have to give you? Drink your wine, bless your beard, and close your eyes. Even if you die tonight, nothing will change and nothing will be lost.

That is what I said to myself, and I grew calm. I reconciled myself with death every evening on the balcony, and I had forgotten it by the following day. The only incontrovertible truth—that I was mortal—lay beyond my reach. I saw it and understood it, but then I forgot about it, and the struggle for honor and food on the table began afresh each morning.

"What are you thinking about?" Gunilla would often ask. "That I'm going to die," I would reply, as undramatically as possible without really grasping exactly what I meant. Death is constantly present and always incomprehensible.

One beautiful day I would lose her too. I would no longer be able to see her foot sticking out from underneath the covers like the devil's claw in the mornings. She always sleeps that way. With one foot outside the covers.

I would lose my children and grandchildren. It was best to leave first, not to experience more losses. There was already a small graveyard in my heart for the dear departed. My parents, my older brother Giorgos, friends. Sometimes I was angry with them.

My friend Diagoras, for example. We had known each other since we were twelve years old. One day we were sitting in our favorite café, Sonia on Alexandras Avenue in Athens, talking about the theater of which he was the director, his forthcoming projects, and the loneliness that surrounded us day by day. He had had open-heart surgery twice, but he was still alive, still drinking and smoking; our eyes met with inexpressible, sorrowful tenderness. Then we said our goodbyes. He went to work, and I returned to Stockholm.

Giannis Fertis, the third member of our closed circle and a noted actor, called me three months later. Diagoras had departed, not without severe pain. Was I coming to the funeral? "But Giannis, I'm in Sweden," I replied.

That was how it was. I was somewhere else.

I had always been somewhere else, for the past fifty-five years. I asked Giannis to place a flower on the coffin on my behalf. Not only did he do that, but he also made sure he included me in the short speech he gave. He wasn't in the habit of making speeches. I am translating it here, because one of the longest and most beautiful chapters of our lives came to an end with Diagoras's death.

We had known one another since the first year of high school. The remarkable thing was that we knew exactly what we wanted to do in life. Diagoras wanted to become a director, Giannis an actor, and I a writer. Art was our god back then.

I read the speech late one evening in a taverna in Athens. Marina, Giannis's wife, presented me with a lovely icon she had painted. It showed "the three boys by the fireside," three young Christian martyrs who had been burned alive. I was already deeply moved and felt that heaven was bending over us when this letter was placed in my hand.

My friend Diagoras,

You took your leave early on Wednesday morning, and I want to apologize for the fact that I had already forgotten you that evening. I went to the theater, I asked the girl in the box office if we had an audience, I played my role as if nothing had happened, and when I got home I forgot you again, because I watched the football on TV.

I know that I will remember you less and less often during the years I have left to live, just like

my mother, my father, and my brother. But when
I do remember you I will travel back in time, to
the days when we were in school. When at the age
of seventeen, together with our beloved friend and
classmate Thodoris Kallifatides, we sneaked out of
our homes just after midnight, when our parents
had fallen asleep, to go to one of the two cafés on
Alexandras Avenue that stayed open all night. We
drank coffee and smoked. But the most important
thing of all: we talked only about theater.

We crept back into our houses, making sure
that our parents didn't catch us. We slept for three
or four hours, then went to school together in the
morning, unless of course I was playing truant.

I had to pause to catch my breath. I remembered our devotion, our passion, that irrepressible desire to achieve something.

Where had it gone?

Diagoras had all of that until he died. Plus the ability to get mad.

That was why your friends Thodoris and
I conspired to make you angry. I can still see the
picture in my mind: you are walking twenty yards

in front of us, refusing to have anything to do with
us while we laugh behind you.
    Farewell, my friend!

I remembered that picture too.

I am ashamed that I wasn't at Diagoras's funeral, but I'm sure he would forgive me. Because he was capable of forgiveness too, and one day we will follow him, although this time we won't be laughing.

There was also the question of those who would lose me. The person who would have experienced the greatest pain—my mother—was already gone. Gunilla would grieve for a while, there would be days when she would call out to tell me that dinner was ready even though I could no longer eat, and the children might remember the jokes they hated, or the times when I used to cheat in our card games, or when we all used to engage in wrestling bouts on the double bed. But time eases all sorrow, the present takes up all of our time, the dead become more dead with each passing day until nothing remains but the tradition of celebrating a birthday, discreetly raising a little flag on the balcony. "Dad would have been ninety-five today," Gunilla would say before everyone drank coffee and ate cake.

And what about the grandchildren? My grandson had already talked about the matter at length. He was thirteen years old. We had been on an excursion to Fårö, and I had told the children about my schools, including the high school teacher who called me "garbage" because I was so skinny. They laughed, and then my grandson said, "Grandpa, I'm going to give a speech at your funeral. Everyone else will talk about your books, but I haven't read a single line that you've written, except for the little verses on our Christmas presents. But you're the funniest person I know. That's what I'm going to say."

That's what he said, and it brought tears to my eyes.

Emigration is a kind of partial suicide. You don't die, but a great deal dies within you. Not least, the language. That's why I am more proud of not having forgotten my Greek than of having learned Swedish. The latter was a matter of necessity, the former an act of love, a victory over indifference and forgetfulness.

I had thrown a black stone behind me, as they say in my village when a person has decided to leave everything. And yet I couldn't forget. I missed Greece and Greek more and more. In a drawer lay a few letters from Maria, who had been my dearest love before I left the country. I took them out and read them slowly. Not to recall that youthful love, but to enjoy her Greek, and because she had hidden a ticking time bomb in my brain.

"Come back, we still have many fine walks to take," she said when we were no longer lovers but something even more valuable. We were the best of friends. I read her letters in order to taste my language. When all my longing had deserted me, I still missed my language. The feeling didn't go away, but grew stronger over time.

I could see it in my everyday life too. I would call my friend Giorgos on the flimsiest pretext just to exchange a few words in Greek, even if the language was the result of a distillation after several decades in Sweden.

"How's it going, Boss?"

He's a mechanic, and looked after my car too.

"Crap! I'm sitting here dying!"

In fact the doctors couldn't find anything wrong with him, but he could no longer walk unaided, and he was unable to drive. He's the best driver I've ever seen in my life. Guaranteed. Half an inch is enough for him to overtake at full speed. His workshop had a very narrow entrance. Most of us were capable of driving in, but reversing out was a different story. We left it to him, and he went for it as if he were on a freeway. But these days he didn't drive anymore. His last love—an olive green Saab that he had modified and improved to 350 horsepower— stood trapped in a garage. He went there at regular intervals to visit it.

Giorgos has a big heart, but his soul struggled to accept the situation.

"Sell it and you'll have peace of mind," I would say to him. We had gone to the garage together several times. The car was covered in a tarpaulin to stop it from gathering dust. It actually shone.

"Nobody wants it. It uses too much fuel."

In this Saab he used to drive down to Germany, where he would play cat and mouse with all the flashy Mercedes and BMWs as they attempted in vain to overtake him.

"Take it easy, my Giorgos," his wife would beg.

"You don't know what they did to us during the war," he would reply, putting his foot down so that his made-in-Sweden olive green Pegasus flew away from his pursuers.

All that was over now. When he started talking about selling his workshop, saying that he was tired of it all, he held up his hands.

"They can't do it anymore."

That wasn't entirely true. Things weren't the same as before, when he could tear the phone book in half, but shaking hands with him was still a painful experience.

We had met back in 1966, when he ran his workshop with another Giorgos. For some reason he called himself the Worker and this other Giorgos the Employer. I called Worker Giorgos "Boss" and Employer Giorgos "Giorgos." They had become an institution among the Greeks in Stockholm, and I thought the world of them both.

Since I left Greece I had subconsciously been searching for a big brother. Someone who was stronger, more courageous, more secure. It wasn't that easy to find someone more sensible, if I may say so myself, and it's probably best to do so because no one else is going to say it.

During the dictatorship, this workshop had become a hub for democratically minded Greeks in Stockholm, and Employer Giorgos revealed unsuspected talents. Within a short time he became one of the most influential leaders of the fight for democracy in Greece. After the fall of the dictatorship he continued to work politically in Sweden; he left the workshop and never returned.

Worker Giorgos was left to run the business on his own, and moved closer to the city center. We would go there when we had nothing better to do. There was always coffee on offer. We chatted, and the cabdrivers told amusing stories about their night shifts.

"Stockholm is Stockholm until one o'clock in the morning. After that it turns into Sodom and Gomorrah."

People who didn't have a car, had no intention of buying a car, and couldn't afford a car also came to the workshop. The guy from the East, for example, an elderly Turk with big, gentle eyes, a soft voice, and a persistent cough, which was probably the reason he had been pensioned off early. He lived alone, read a little, and didn't have much to say, but it was clear that he enjoyed spending time with Giorgos, who had designated him Principal Coffee Maker.

The Turk reminded me of my maternal grand-mother. He sat exactly as she did, straight backed with his hands clasped, his gaze bright and steady. You had the feeling that nothing could disrupt their absolute composure, which I like to call "the strength of the weak," a realization that it is possible to endure anything, that you are ready for whatever may happen at any moment. These people know that they can't rule the world, but they can rule their own fear.

Then we had the Jew. No one knew if he was actually a Jew, but that's what we'd called him because he was a well-educated man, unlike the rest of us. It was rumored that he'd been a judge, and he was brought in occasionally to solve minor practical or ideological conflicts. He too lived alone, but he had "his dead companions," as he put it.

There were also the Single Ladies—elderly women who brought their defective cars to Giorgos's workshop, partly because his prices were low, partly because he sometimes refused to take any money at all if he suspected that the customer in question was in a bit of a fix financially. One of these ladies once took a photograph of Giorgos and me because we looked "so beautiful together" with our graying heads. How the hell could he let her pay after that?

None of us wanted Giorgos to retire, but he found a Yugoslav, sold the workshop, put the money in the bank, and went home.

"I'm going to wash my hands," he said.

A week later the first symptoms appeared. The odd pain here and there, some worse than others, dizziness, tiredness, his tongue felt thick, and he found it difficult to talk. We had lunch together one day. I had never seen him in a shirt and jacket, and hardly recognized him without his overalls. He came toward me smiling, but his footsteps were cautious, almost anxious.

He insisted that lunch was on him.

"Eat up, you need to put on some weight, you poor old scribbler," he said.

"What do the doctors say, Boss?"

"They say nothing. They talk about the weather. Tell me I've inhaled too many exhaust fumes, that I'll soon get better."

He didn't get better.

The conclusion was that we grow old, and the best we can do is to grow old while we're working. I should have learned my lesson, but I didn't. Instead of continuing to write at all costs, I had given up.

When I was twenty-five years old, I asked myself how I should live my life, and the answer was: *Leave*. That was exactly what I did. Now, at over seventy-five years old, I was faced with the same question: How should I live the years that remained of my life? More and more frequently, the answer was: *Go back*.

The days passed, and it was June. The city slowly emptied. It was time for us to go to our summer place on Gotland. We had been there every summer since 1971. In other words, I had plenty of material if I wished to draw comparisons.

Comparisons with what? The dizzying speed of the consumer society. For the first few years we owned a used Ford Taunus, if anyone remembers that model. We loaded it up with everything we needed—and we needed virtually everything, from sheets to kitchen equipment. We transported an entire home, and it worked well. Then we had our son, followed three years later by our daughter, and Gunilla just had to take her favorite potted plants with her. Which was fine. As the years passed, we bought things for our summer cottage, we almost had a complete home there, and we also acquired a bigger car. That too was crammed full, and the children sat with potted plants on their laps. A few years later we bought another car, and now both cars were packed to bursting. The children grew up and no longer accompanied us to Gotland. Gunilla and I traveled there in separate cars, still shifting just as much stuff back and forth.

We had two fully equipped homes, but the anxiety-laden trips continued. At the beginning we didn't even have a can of beer with us, but as time went on we took wines we couldn't find on Gotland, whiskey and schnapps for those dinners on summer nights, even more potted plants, various treats we would miss, suits and dresses for a range of social events that seemed to keep increasing in number. We scampered around to christenings, weddings, and funerals, we invited people to dinner, we hurried off to dinner elsewhere. The somewhat desolate headland where we lived was no longer so desolate.

We didn't have a vacation, we simply swapped the places where we lived and our winter life for our summer life. We always had guests. My wife likes to have people around her. I prefer to be alone. I also get tired very quickly, glancing at the clock even in the company of good friends.

For that reason we built a small house intended as a studio for me. On the shore one day I found a piece of wood, polished by the sea until it resembled marble. Gunilla wrote THEO'S HOUSE on it, and I hung it above the pretty pale blue door, then went inside and settled down at the computer.

I sat there for three hours; not one word was written. It felt as if my true "self" was hanging over the door, and I was no more than a pale imitation.

I took down the sign and went back inside with my true "self" under my arm. After fifteen minutes I had filled a page.

That's how a simple truth was revealed to me on that occasion. When you start to safeguard your writing, when you start to be the *author*, when you hang yourself up on the wall, it's already over. Writing works in the same way as a spring. You can create fantastic adornments all around it, you can construct a beautiful fountain, plant lovely trees. None of this will make the water flow. It is the pressure from deep within the darkness of the earth's interior which makes that happen.

This doesn't mean that as an author you should fold your arms and wait until the egg is boiled. You have to work all the time, learn to appreciate other writers, which most of us are disinclined to do. You have to learn to hold back, not to step into every shop window that presents itself.

In this way our visits to the island provided an ideal training camp for me. I would take my notepad and stroll down to my deserted beach. Everything around me carried on as usual. I might scare away a little lizard now and again, but that was all.

There, with no witnesses apart from the sea and the sky, I tried to write as best I could. Occasionally it went really well.

But not anymore. My spring had dried up. I could have erected a mausoleum around it. That would have been no help at all. And close to my beach small luxury houses for the young and wealthy were being built, there were plans for restaurants and concerts, exhibitions and goodness knows what else. Large yachts with laughing passengers on board fought for space with noisy motor launches, from which no laughter could be heard.

The place had changed direction. It was now facing consumerism and entertainment. This change was even more noticeable in Fårösund, the nearest built-up area, which was already a functioning community when we first went there in 1971.

There was a school, a library, a clinic, a doctor, three banks, three grocery stores, a regular bus service plus a school bus, three restaurants, and a fine old hotel where the local Rotary Club held its meetings. There was even a bookshop.

The linchpin of the economy was the Coastal Artillery Regiment, which was stationed there, along with the Bungenäs artillery training facility on the land adjoining our property. I wasn't overimpressed with military discipline. There was all kinds of activity going on around the entrance to the base, and they drove their military vehicles at full speed along the dirt track into the village. All in all there were almost six hundred professional soldiers plus fifty civilian administrators, tradesmen, and mechanics living in Fårösund.

In those days Gotland and Fårö were key military zones. There were signs everywhere forbidding unauthorized access, the taking of photographs, and so on. Foreigners were also completely banned from certain areas, and from buying land.

We bought the house in Gunilla's name, but I had to have permission to be there. I could obtain a permit from the commander of the regiment, who lived in the most beautiful house in the village. Gunilla and I went to see him, and everything was sorted out after a few minutes' pleasant conversation. I think he decided to trust me when he heard that I'd done my military service in Greece, so I hadn't deserted my country but had in fact served it for twenty-eight months.

Fårösund's social life had acquired a khaki hue. There was a hierarchy that everyone respected. The only threat came from the "08s," as the locals referred to the tourists because of Stockholm's area code.

Gotland had become fashionable, even though Fårö was the real magnet. More and more outsiders were buying or building summer homes. The ferry from Nynäshamn to Visby was crawling with famous people and celebrities. I once saw Olof Palme sitting cross-legged with his sons, eating sandwiches made by his wife, Lisbet. He was already prime minister back then, but there were no bodyguards, there was no car waiting on the quayside. He was simply a Swedish father on holiday with his family. Sweden was still innocent. It wouldn't stay that way.

The Vietnam War woke my generation. Demonstrations in the cities spread to rural areas. A peace movement was founded on the island, and one of its demands was demilitarization—all military units must be moved elsewhere. We organized marches with our kids on our backs, we produced posters and banners, the take-up was moderate and the atmosphere pleasant, it was a kind of revolutionary vacation, so to speak.

One evening, after yet another short march, we gathered at a newly opened restaurant and Olof Palme came along to say a few words. This remarkable politician had already read my debut poetry collection and quoted a verse from it, not to praise it but to express his opposition. When I look at that verse today I blush with embarrassment, but at the time I absolutely believed in what I had written. Sometimes I think the point of old age is to be embarrassed about one's youth.

Palme made me happy that evening anyway. My new country was prepared to listen to what I had to say.

The war in Vietnam ended. The left suddenly turned into a bullfighter without a bull. The route from street demonstrations to the living room proved surprisingly easy. We locked ourselves in, looked after our home and family, learned how to cook complicated dishes and how to choose wine, got divorced in order to make a fresh start. In the past we didn't get divorced even if there was a good reason; now we got divorced for any reason at all. We had been fellow citizens—now we were individuals.

The international détente and the steady increase in social projects made it necessary to implement cuts, including within the defense budget. The regiment at Fårösund was to be disbanded, and a new act in our comedy began. We went back out onto the streets, but this time we were demanding that the regiment remain. The whole of northern Gotland would go under without it. A large number of shops would close, as would the banks and the school, we would lose our doctor, rents would fall, and the value of our properties would be significantly reduced.

The minister for defense didn't mince his words: "We didn't listen to you last time. We're not going to listen to you this time either." That's what he said, and that's what happened.

The regiment was disbanded and all of our fears were realized; unemployment rose. But people didn't sit around lamenting their fate. Fårösund survived: new small businesses started up; the barracks became hotels, restaurants, youth hostels; a folk high school opened; tourism increased. Unemployment went down, and after a while it was impossible to get hold of a tradesman; people were brought in from our neighboring countries or even farther afield. The military air base was also taken over, and a newly established aviation company offered direct flights to Stockholm for the young and wealthy. Men and women at the younger end of middle age learned to fly small planes or hunt. The residents of this formerly ascetic Protestant community complained that they carried Luther on their backs, which was why they couldn't live life in any other way except when they visited Spain or Greece as tourists. "You know how to live," they would say to me; I was still the only Greek in the village.

Luther was forgotten now. The younger generation might just about have heard of him. They certainly didn't carry him on their backs. The community changed from the collective responsibility of its residents to the equally collective flight from that responsibility.

It was very rare for someone in a position of authority to admit that a mistake had been made, or that anyone was responsible for such an error. The Greek expression for indifference is "It's raining somewhere else." That wasn't really appropriate because it rains everywhere in Sweden, but the sentiment was the same. The responsibility always lay elsewhere. Past blunders and miscalculations also had a legendary ability to survive. It just wasn't possible to put them right. The municipalization or decentralization of the education system destroyed our elementary schools, everyone knows that. But it hasn't been changed, and it probably never will be. A number of private schools of varying degrees of competence and diligence have been set up, but the result of all this is that the children of less-well-off families will attend worse and worse schools. Decentralization was a crime against the democratic contract, and so far no one has apologized. And they never will.

These changes also made their mark, albeit on a smaller scale, in Fårösund. Some things didn't survive. The three banks became one, the school bus disappeared, the three grocery stores also went down to one, and the bookshop was gone for good.

Other changes were also noticeable, for example, the relationship between the local population and the tourists. In the 1970s there was a certain warmth, a friendliness, which was gradually replaced by mutual distrust. The tourists were perceived as parasites, but the locals wanted their money. Meanwhile, the tourists didn't really want anything to do with the locals, but they needed their services.

It was a paradoxical process. Words such as "conscience," "duty," "responsibility" were distorted or mocked, or simply disappeared. Sweden had discovered the carefree life. In my homeland, Greece, people strove to be like my second country, Sweden, where people wanted to live as they did in Greece. In Greece they dreamed of the Swedish model, while in Sweden they dreamed of the Greek lack of any kind of model.

We had the same problem at home. Gunilla tried to teach me her theory about organization, which I gradually realized lay at the heart of the Swedish model.

"Before you can do something, you must do something else first."

That was how she ran our everyday lives. Let me give you some examples. Before you can open a window, you must remove all the potted plants from the windowsill. Before you can load up the car, you must wash it. Before you make the bed, you must air the sheets. And so on. But she never forgot anything.

I, on the other hand, always forgot something, even if it was nothing major. My boots, maybe, or the novel I was reading. Gunilla advised me to make lists. So I made lists, but I forgot where I'd put them.

However, my forgetfulness reached a whole new level when I made the decision to step aside. My brain was like a clock that had stopped at the wrong time.

It turned out that in addition to several items of clothing and medication, I had forgotten all my notes and material relating to a past project, plus my Swedish and Greek dictionaries, which had been my companions throughout the years. Without them I was helpless.

My reaction was not what you would call normal. I didn't try to work out a way of getting the things I lacked. On the contrary. I accepted it, as yet further proof that I ought not to write. My forgetfulness was not a coincidence but evidence that I was distancing myself from myself. If I didn't remember something, it was because it wasn't worth remembering. If I didn't write something, it was because it wasn't worth writing.

"That's a fine start to the summer," I said to Gun-illa. She hadn't forgotten anything, but her left knee was causing her problems.

"It's all going downhill," I added. She didn't reply but went out to inspect the devastation. The rabbits had taken everything, but my beautiful Ispahan roses had survived.

We need to grow thorns if we're going to survive, I said to myself. I didn't grow thorns, but a few days later I discovered a patch on the left side of my head, on the temple. I touched it; I could feel it, but there was nothing to see.

Gunilla was summoned and immediately delivered her diagnosis.

"It's the patch of forgetfulness," she said, and went on to explain that this was common in *men of my age*. Women, on the other hand, were spared.

That wasn't all. I suddenly developed a growth on the palm of my right hand. It didn't hurt, but I was bothered by the fact that I could feel it all the time. I spoke to a doctor I knew, a younger woman. She reassured me. It was nothing to worry about. It was very common in *men of my age*. There was no need for surgery, it wouldn't get any worse.

That made me feel better. I sat down at the computer to see if anything would happen, but there was nothing. Not one single word popped up. I kept scratching the patch of forgetfulness and thought it was getting bigger and bigger.

Fortunately, I picked up Stefan Zweig's *The World of Yesterday*. It was his last book. He took his own life in Brazil in February 1942, together with his much younger wife. Why? one might ask. His world of yesterday was gone and would never return. Hitler had destroyed it, once and for all.

The World of Yesterday is an outstanding book, written in a musical, gently lilting prose that is simply irresistible.

It gave me great consolation. The aging Zweig lived a lonely, isolated life in Petrópolis, Brazil. He couldn't return to his Europe, and yet he found the strength to write his best book.

What did I have to complain about? My situation wasn't remotely dramatic. I could visit my homeland at any time. I also had children and grandchildren. How can you kill yourself and leave such a legacy behind?

The first visitors were our daughter and her husband. We were particularly pleased because we didn't see them very often. They lived in the Tuscany of Skåne, in the lovely hills around Lake Börringe. I have never in my life seen such "erotic" earth. It shone in the sun like one of Zorn's bathers with their voluptuous thighs; it perspired. If you pushed a dry twig into that earth, you would have a tree a week later.

They stayed with us for about ten days, and it was a great success. Then our son turned up with his children. The house was full, even though the children soon disappeared all day long with the friends they had made the previous summer.

Our son gave us a pear tree as a gift, and he planted it himself to replace the previous pear, which was old and sickly. It had been the most beautiful tree in the garden once upon a time; it bore plenty of fruit and had a lush leaf canopy. I must also mention that I love pears so much that I like to refer to the forbidden fruit from the Tree of Knowledge as a pear rather than an apple. In the late summer when the pears were ripe and the dew made them shimmer like little suns, I would pick one every morning and take a big bite. The juice would run down my chin, and it felt like the taste of the world, of life.

My son dug away, bare-chested, while I sat and watched, lost in thoughts of my mother and father. They had visited this Gotland garden, my mother with her fairy-tale little slippers and my father with his golden pajamas. He tried to teach the children Greek, without much success. My mother didn't bother. Her whole body was a language with many names and verbs.

The children left and the house was empty, but our days were not. Our social life took over. We ate and drank in various places, with plenty of drinking songs.

I have written this before, but not everyone has read my books, unfortunately, so I will write it again:

Greeks sing when they drink, Swedes sing so they can drink. Over the years it has become an enjoyable habit to collect synonyms for the songs that traditionally accompany the drinking of schnapps. My two favorites are *jamare* and *tuting*.

I don't know if there's any other language in the world with such a rich imagination in this area.

Things were good, but the emptiness inside me was growing. The days seemed endless without my writing. But I couldn't write. I went for long walks on my own, found my way back to places that I loved, for example the English cemetery on Fårö. It dates from the time of the Crimean War, 1854. The gravestones are illegible; the wind and rain have obliterated the inscriptions. A number of British seamen who died in a cholera epidemic are buried there in a plot marked with heavy chains, as if there was a risk it might blow away in the bitter east winds from Estonia. I also used to visit the fortress from the same period and the same war, which is still there, surrounded by rusty medieval anticavalry defense barriers. On other occasions I took the car and drove inland to see stone circles and ancient graves. These peepholes into history affect me like powerful drugs. I arrive there with one head and leave with a different one.

I went to my secret shore, where I was almost always completely alone, but my brain didn't open up as it used to do. I was looking at the landscape, but I wasn't seeing it. In the afternoons I sat in the recently opened café Maffen with the world's best espresso, and my heart was heavy with a sorrow I didn't understand.

What was it that had come between me and the words? We had been friends for so long. Not anymore.

Friends and acquaintances often asked why I hadn't bought myself a little place in Greece. My answers varied; I would say that I didn't want to be a tourist in my homeland, that I didn't want to stop feeling homesick, that I didn't want to put Greece in a pot like a flower. They were all true. As was the most important reason: I had found my Greece on Gotland.

There was the same dual light from the sea and the sky, the same darkness, the same windblown pine trees, the same sandstone and limestone. The island also had a history that was still visible. Fårösund had been the naval base for the British and French fleet during the Crimean War. The barracks were still there and had been converted into restaurants or hostels.

Sometimes we had dinner there, with the sea right in front of us. To put it briefly, I liked Fårösund very much.

The days passed and I tried to stick to my routines, because the emptiness within me was growing alarmingly. I read the newspaper as pedantically as possible. I also made certain adjustments. I switched on the radio in the mornings, which would have been unthinkable before. I also tried to change my breakfast, but that was harder than I thought. Every day seemed virtually endless. I took up more activities, went to the gym in Fårösund, pumped iron, went on the rowing machine, groaned and generally behaved in a way that was completely out of character. There were several of us, all slightly older ladies and gentlemen.

One of the ladies, who was also very easy to get on with, had read some of my books, including my crime novels. One day she opened a door that I'd never seen open before and announced, "This would be a good place to hide a dead body!"

But she knew who I was, which was the main thing to the old Greek that I am. That's what the Greek dreams of: for everyone to know who he is. I was reminded of a minor quarrel in a taverna. My brother, who had invited me for a meal, wasn't happy, but the waiter stood up to him. At that point my brother played his final ace.

"Do you know who you're talking to?" he asked, eyebrows knitted together in a frown.

"Yes," the waiter replied. "You used to be my teacher."

We had a fine evening after that.

I had a fine day at the gym too.

When I got home that day I sat down at the computer and wrote a sentence that was buzzing around in my head like a horsefly. I've actually forgotten what it was, but I felt it was necessary to do something with it. It was a great relief, as if the troll that had struck me dumb had finally taken pity on me.

I also wanted to make this sentence public in some way, so I opened a Twitter account and let it fly out into space.

Five minutes later I had ten alerts. By the evening there were a hundred people "following" me. Appetite comes when you eat, as they say in Greece. It was an immediate form of communication, there was no need for an editor or a publisher, there was no censorship apart from my own. I could say whatever I wanted, and it would reach an audience.

I have to admit that until then I hadn't been very positively inclined toward these new fashions, so-called social media. I changed my mind. Of course there were plenty of indifferent messages, but there were also those that meant something, that taught me something.

If Jesus were alive today, he would be on social media, I thought. "Love one another as I have loved you." Is there a better tweet?

I had found a homeopathic model. I wrote on Twitter because I couldn't write as I used to do.

And so the summer passed almost as usual, while Fårösund continued to change. When we first went there, there were 1,060 inhabitants. I was the only foreigner. The population had been declining steadily ever since, and in the summer of 2015, the figure was 856, but I was no longer the only foreigner.

First came the Romanian Roma. One morning we saw a young Roma woman sitting outside the ICA store. All of a sudden. It was impossible to keep the poor away. Then nine unaccompanied boys were placed in the community. I often saw them at the gym, where they reverted to being children for a little while. They teased one another, compared their muscles, laughed. But when they wandered aimlessly through the streets, they were no longer children. They were foreigners, they stuck close together as if to protect themselves.

I remembered that feeling from my early years in Sweden. I stuck close to the buildings, kept my head down.

Who knows what these boys will write one day? I thought.

Then came more refugees. The people of Fårösund turned out to possess great kindness and generosity. The world was changing. Everything was changing, apart from the bad luck that had joined me for the summer. Mice chewed through the wiring and packing in my car, my computer gave up the ghost, taking with it five years of manuscripts, addresses, photographs, letters, documents, and so on. I had copies, of course, but it took two painful weeks to restore my files. Worst of all, I nearly burned down my house. I forgot about a pan on the stove. Fortunately, I had also forgotten to lock the door behind me, so when my neighbor saw the smoke, he was able to go in and put out the fire.

What was happening to me?

Which god had I angered?

One afternoon toward the end of the summer, when the birds began to fly south, I saw one traveling all alone. It had lost its flock, yet still it continued its journey across the empty sky. The direction was imprinted on its little brain.

What about me? Was there a direction imprinted within me?

Without being conscious of it, I was thinking more and more frequently about Greece. Maybe that was the problem. With each passing day I lost a bit more of my homeland. I had seen the same thing in others in my situation. They shrank in an alien environment, apparently with no real reason. They were successful, they had their own summer residence back home, they went there as often as they could. But it wasn't enough, and in the end they went home for good.

"Come back, we still have many fine walks to take." That was what my dear friend Maria had said. Maybe that was what was missing from my life. Those walks in Athens, the ones I hadn't yet taken.

My mother's apartment happened to be empty at that particular time. The financial crisis had forced the tenants to move out. When would such an opportunity arise again? My brother Stelios, who took care of the place, promised to keep it available for me.

I spoke to Gunilla, and she liked the idea.

III

We landed in Athens ten days later, in the middle of September. It was ten o'clock at night. There was no sign of my suitcase. The luggage carousel stopped. I was about to go and look for an attendant when it started moving again. Gunilla and I held our breath. After a minute or so my suitcase appeared all by itself, as if it were teasing me. For the first time in my life I hated a suitcase.

"You're in luck," Gunilla informed me.

What can you say?

One of the best things about Athens airport is that there's always a cab. We quickly found one, loaded our bags in the trunk, and got in. Gunilla asked me what I'd done with my case. I'd left it on the sidewalk. Fortunately, it was still there.

"Gyzi Square," I said to the driver.

I hadn't given that address for several years, not since my mother died, in fact. That was where she lived. That was where she died. That was where Gunilla and I were going now. In the car we talked about my parents, about my father and his golden pajamas, and about my mother's cookies.

The fog inside me lifted slightly.

And still I dropped my wallet on the street without noticing. The driver picked it up and gave it back to me.

"You're lucky it was me," he said.

Gunilla flared up. "One of these days you'll forget all about me too! Are you in love?" she snapped.

It would be wonderful if I was, but I wasn't. "You don't fall in love *at my age*," I declared with a certain pride in my wisdom.

Stelios was waiting in the apartment to give us the keys and various instructions about the hot water and so on. He had also bought some food for breakfast the following morning. Then he hurried off home, because he wasn't feeling too well.

We were left alone. I looked around. The kitchen table, my mother's double bed. What had I expected from these two rooms after all these years? I felt nothing. We quickly unpacked and went down to the square. All the shops were open. We took a short stroll to stretch our legs, then sat down for something to eat. We had both been longing for the same things: cooked dandelion greens, feta cheese, and fried herring. They didn't have the fish. Or any retsina. My wife shook her head.

"The fish I can understand, but not being able to get a glass of retsina in Greece? Greece without retsina is like love without kisses."

I thought kisses without love would be worse, but I said something else. I said that I didn't feel anything at all. Gunilla wondered what I'd expected to feel.

"I don't know. Something. I expected something to open up inside me. A thought or a memory, but there's nothing."

She wasn't particularly concerned.

"It will come when it comes. I'm happy anyway. Tomorrow we will drink coffee on the balcony. You'll just have to be patient."

The traffic around the square was beginning to thin out. It was well after midnight. The bakery pulled down its iron grille. The waiter brought our bill.

"How's business?" I asked.

"What business?" he responded.

There were more stray cats than customers. Emaciated, restless, nervous, they cautiously edged closer, waiting for something to eat. Gunilla gave the first one a tidbit, and more appeared.

It was very late, but not for the Athenians. They stayed where they were, including the young couples who were in love, kissing and cuddling on the benches in the square, speaking different languages. I picked out Russian, Albanian, Greek, Arabic, but there were more.

I couldn't help remembering my teenage years beneath the trees in this square. And yet it all felt so far away, as if those years had never happened. I thought about what Philip Roth had said—that you can't write when the memories disappear.

It's easily understandable, and that was my problem. I remembered, but the memories were no longer relevant.

They had no life. They were turning into photographs. I was turning into a photograph of myself.

I looked at my wife, perhaps seeking help. She was finishing the last drops of her wine, her head tipped back. Her throat was shiny with sweat, and a flash went off in my head. She had just given birth to our first child. She was drenched in sweat, but she looked so incredibly happy as she held that little person in her arms.

"I shall do this again," she said.

I had never forgotten that, and I never will. We've lived together since the fall of 1968, and I was grateful for that night in the square.

At my age it's sensible to keep your woman by your side.

"Aren't you going to smoke your cigarette?" I asked.

She has smoked one cigarette a day for several years now, always in the evening after dinner. Just one. My father drank one glass of red wine for as long as I could recall. Just one. Never two. I admire people like that, but I also fear them a little. What tenacity must a person have to keep a promise that he or she could easily break without anyone uttering a word of reproach?

"I am—on Mama's balcony."

My mother's balcony had acquired a life of its own for my wife too. We had spent so many hours there, drunk so many cups of coffee, my mother had read our fortunes in the coffee grounds. I thought about it over and over again in the hope that something would be brought to life inside me, but nothing happened. I had turned to stone.

In the past I could always feel it as soon as I landed at Athens airport. My lungs expanded, I breathed in my homeland along with the aviation fuel. But this time, nothing happened.

I was haunted by a sense of being in the wrong place all the time; this was clearly a result of my inability to write. I was like a ship that had lost its buoyancy.

The same thing had occurred in Sweden too. I withdrew without being aware of it. Suddenly, in the middle of a conversation with people I liked and valued, I fled. If you entered a room crowded with a hundred people and saw a skinny man standing alone in a corner, that was me.

Maybe that's the price of living in a foreign country. It's not just that you live a different life from the one you've left behind, it's the fact that the alienation makes you an alien.

Who or what would lift this curse from my shoulders so that I could once again become what I wanted to be: a human being among other human beings?

A few months earlier I had received an email from my village, Molai. It came from the principal of the local high school, Olympia Lampoussi. I had heard that surname before. A forester called Lampoussi had created the beautiful avenue of aromatic eucalyptus trees outside the village. Olympia's question was very specific and completely unexpected.

She and her colleagues wanted to name the school after me. Did I have anything against the proposal? She couldn't imagine that I would, but one of her colleagues had said that I must be asked first. "It's possible that he might not like the idea," he had said.

It was theoretically possible, but I did like the idea—very much. I hadn't expected such a gesture. My village had already honored me by giving a street my name. I hadn't seen it, however, except in photographs.

I immediately thought of my father, who had been a teacher in that same village. The news wouldn't reach him, but I knew he would have been happy and proud. "We never give up," he used to say. His death didn't prevent me from experiencing his happiness and pride. To hell with death!

I wanted to see my street. And my school, even more so! My friend Maria, who was no longer alive, had once said to me, "You, my friend, would run to your own execution if they promised to put up a sign about it on that very spot."

She wasn't wrong. I have nothing against formal honors. Quite the reverse. That was why I wrote. To have my name on a street in my village, to have a school named after me, to carry on existing. I'm sure that authors and artists felt the same way before we and the rest of society were browbeaten by the market. Eternity was no longer fashionable.

Greece and the Greeks were once more struggling to avoid defeat, as so many times in the past. The German Occupation during the Second World War, the civil war that followed, the mass emigration—these were the experiences that had shaped my generation. Virtually all of us had deaths to mourn, injustices that embittered us, abandoned dreams rotting in our souls. But none of this could be compared with the spiritual impoverishment we had experienced recently.

Greece was humiliated on a daily basis in the European press. We had suffered before, but back then we had the sympathy of our fellow human beings; right was on our side. The situation was completely different now. I saw cartoons that reminded me of the posters Dr. Goebbels had distributed all over Greece back in the day, depicting the Greeks as long-armed apes. My heart bled. Once more I thought of my father.

"We didn't win our freedom in order to become slaves to our habits." That was what he used to say when he was trying to get my brother and me to give up smoking. He didn't succeed. Instead we seduced our mother into our bad ways, and she would smoke the odd cigarette.

This time Greece was not paying for its old habits, but selling itself in order to hold on to them.

It was taking some time for the minister of education to make a decision on the school's change of name.

I could understand that. Who had time to deal with that kind of thing when the whole country was teetering on the brink? But the teachers in the school would be pleased if I paid them a visit. The students read my books, and this summer they would be staging a tragedy by Aeschylus.

"Dear stranger," wrote the principal, "if for no other reason, please come to hear beautiful Greek."

It sounded like an invocation. I couldn't resist such an invitation, so I promised to go.

I lay beside my wife on the bed in which my mother had died, totally unmoved. I have become utterly soulless, I thought.

As always Gunilla read for a while before switching off the light. She kissed me gently in the darkness and we said good night.

Everything was just the same as usual, even though nothing was.

The following morning I was woken by a noise that sounded as if someone was trying to start a reluctant engine. It was the doves. It wasn't even five o'clock. I made myself a cup of coffee, then went and sat in my magical place—on my mother's balcony—and listened to the city waking up.

I remembered the first time I met Yannis Ritsos, one of the great Greek poets. I was working with Bengt Holmqvist and Östen Sjöstrand on a translation of one of Ritsos's later poems, almost all written during his time on the island of Leros, to which he was exiled by the military junta that seized power in 1967. He had been seriously ill, yet still he worked nonstop. He didn't have much paper, so he wrote very short poems, sometimes only a few lines.

I loved those poems. Bengt and Östen, who had seen a very rough translation, loved them even more and promised to produce a polished version.

That was also why I went to see Ritsos as soon as possible. He welcomed me into his three-room apartment in one of the unremarkable blocks behind the train station from which I had begun the journey toward my future in Sweden, once upon a time.

The room where Ritsos worked overlooked a school-yard. During recess you could hear the wild shouts of the children. But you could hear all the other sounds too. Trains slowing down or laboriously starting up, cars, street traders, particularly one selling watermelons, who roared like a latter-day Stentor: "I will slaughter them all, I will stab them all!" It wasn't as bad as it sounded. The point was that he was prepared to split open his water-melons so that the customer could see the ripe red flesh.

I asked Ritsos if he wasn't disturbed by the noise. No, quite the reverse, he liked it. Particularly in the mornings when he would sit on the balcony to see and hear *his city* wake up.

That was the time for his poetry—the early morning. The rest of the day was given over to the prose writers. He didn't put it that way, but that was how I remembered it as I sat on my mother's balcony. Maybe that was what I ought to do. Start again from the beginning. Find the very first morning.

I learned a lot from my encounter with Yannis Ritsos. A great deal was forgotten over the years, but not what follows. After much agonizing, I dared to ask him, "Dear master, are you sure we say it that way in Greek?"

He didn't take offense but looked at me pensively, then said a little sadly, "But it's not Greek that's saying it that way. It's me."

What confidence he must have had to come out with such a response. I'm not sure I've ever had it, but even if I did, I lost it when I started writing in Swedish—constantly unsure of myself, worried that I was making mistakes, that you didn't say it that way in Swedish. I wrote for over forty years with this sword of Damocles hanging above my head. And I would feel the same even if I were to write for another forty years.

This feeling was preserved and reinforced by the fact that one of the most common arguments is that you don't say *this* but *that* in Swedish. No logical, syntactical, or grammatical reasons were put forward; instead, use of language was invoked. You don't say that in Swedish. Simple. But you can't learn an entire language by heart, I would object with increasing resignation. I am not a monkey. I want to understand why it's *på Gotland*—on Gotland—but not *på England*, which would actually be pretty cool. However, no one has ever come up with an explanation other than that's the way it is in Swedish. I should have followed Ritsos's example. It's me who's speaking. Not Swedish.

The question was what would happen if I tried to write in Greek. What did I remember, what had I forgotten, what had possibly been lost forever? Rediscovering my Greek seemed even more difficult than continuing to live an uncertain life with my Swedish.

Yannis honored me with the gift of a pebble from the shore on which he had written a poem when he was exiled to Leros. He couldn't help saying what he had to say. I treasured that pebble like my own eyes, and yet it was lost when I moved out of my studio. It felt like an omen.

Greek is no longer yours.

Gunilla got up with shining eyes and rosy cheeks; she always sleeps well. She was wearing the blue robe that suits her better than the red one.

We laid out our breakfast on the balcony. Our next-door neighbor was talking to the neighbor on the balcony opposite. We drank coffee between their voices.

A couple of hours later we were enjoying another cup of coffee in the square. Children of all ages were running around in the play area. Once upon a time I played there too. I thought about the gang. Diamantis the First, whom we always called "Rain Shield" because his hair grew straight out from his forehead like a sheet of metal. Diamantis the Second, who was permanently in jail and was known as "Tiger." And Karakatsanis, of course, the equally permanent captain of every team and every game. Doughball, who couldn't even get on the team as goalkeeper. Then little Kostas, the expert dribbler. But that was the end of it. I remembered more friends, but not their names or what we called them. We all had nicknames. I could find them, because they were included in one of my earlier books, but what would be the point of that?

Forgetfulness is a part of life.

Gunilla sat beside me, writing postcards to send home.

I wondered what had happened to all those boys and girls who were still somehow within me like perennials. How many were still alive? Which ones had left us?

The square had changed too. The cozy cafés were now sophisticated coffee shops and bars. The simple restaurant with ready-made food was gone. The barber with his neat black mustache was no longer there. Every time I had visited Athens in the past, I had gone to him for a trim, just for the pleasure of watching him juggle with the scissors as he pondered how to deal with my hair. His fingers were as nimble as those of a top-class pianist.

I wanted everything to be just the same as it used to be. That is the emigrant's drama. The reality he left behind is gone, yet that is what calls to him.

"You can't go back."

My wife looked at me uneasily. "You're talking to yourself."

I denied it.

"And you're crying. Why are you crying?"

"I'm not crying."

But I was crying, without being aware of it. My eyes were being given a thorough watering.

"You can't go back."

Maybe I ought to write about that. It was a fleeting thought, but very comforting.

After a while we took a walk in the stone pine forest of my childhood around the Military Academy. The buildings were now used as courthouses. The first thing that struck me was the smell. I remembered the sharp aroma of pine resin, light and airy, present but not intrusive, like a fleeting caress. Now it stank like an outdoor toilet, a hot, sickening stench that made us recoil. Old newspapers were scattered everywhere, a sign of the homeless people who spent the nights there, impoverished Greeks and refugees. There were empty food cans, used needles and condoms.

The country's economic crisis could be seen in all its nakedness. Terrified stray dogs growled if anyone approached them, while frightened cats scavenged among the piles of rubbish.

The few people who cut through the forest in order to reach the courthouses on the other side moved as quickly as they could. Here and there I saw the type of group I recognized. I had seen them in the square at Medborgarplatsen in Stockholm, often made up of several men and one woman, all equally wretched, sharing a cigarette or a bottle of booze or some kind of narcotic. I had seen them go into the public toilet and lock the door behind them; a little while later I would hear screams and cries for help, or sometimes groans of pleasure.

Poverty, including extreme poverty, was nothing new in my life. I had seen it before, even as a child. On the other side of this forest were the barracks where the

Greek refugees from Asia Minor or the Black Sea lived back then. Their camp was poor, but it wasn't dirty, it wasn't wretched, it wasn't disgusting.

Now poverty was exactly that—disgusting, both in the stone pine forest of my childhood in Athens and in Medborgarplatsen in Stockholm. A war was being waged against these people, and that was something I hadn't understood.

"We're poor, but we have our dignity," my mother used to say. That dignity no longer existed. The poor were no longer people but "problems," a sanitary inconvenience.

I used to say the same thing as my mother. I insisted that both I and everyone else should pull their socks up and get on with things. It appalled me when people allowed themselves to go into a decline; they had a responsibility. That was what I thought.

I was wrong, which was a painful realization. I condemned those who were drowning because they hadn't learned to swim, instead of those who stood by and watched without lifting a finger.

I was one of them.

In the afternoon, quite late, I went out to buy pistachio nuts from Aegina, which are probably the best this earth has to offer, particularly if you eat them with an evening glass of ouzo.

I headed for the usual store, but the good-humored old man who owned it wasn't there. He had been replaced by a short, slim woman of indeterminate age. Her hair was fair, her eyes sparkling with life.

As soon as she saw me she called out: "Welcome— what a handsome young man you are!"

She was overstating the case somewhat, but I can't pretend I wasn't happy with this greeting.

I wanted some pistachio nuts; it would take three minutes at the most. I was there for almost an hour. She told me all about her life. She had emigrated to America when she was young, she had had twenty-five different jobs, she believed in God, the family, and rest. "You have to learn to rest," she said over and over again.

She had four younger sisters and had married them all off while remaining unmarried herself. When her father was dying, he had written to her, "You must marry, otherwise my body will never be received by the earth. I will not turn to dust"—a terrible, harsh fate for an honorable old man.

She left America, came back to Greece, and met the man she married. He was much older than her and a widower, but he was a good man and the earth received her father.

In the middle of this tale, her cell phone rang. It was her elderly husband, who needed oxygen.

"Stay here, I'll be back soon," she said, and hurried off.

Five minutes later she returned, and we continued our conversation. She was eighty-two years old but planned to live to one hundred and eighteen.

"Why one hundred and eighteen?" I wondered.

"First of all, I have to wait until all those who boycott my store because I'm a woman are dead and gone. Look at the bastards!"

She pointed to a group of old men sitting outside the café opposite.

"They grind their teeth every time they walk past this place. They're waiting for my husband to die so they can take over my business, but they're waiting in vain. I'm going to stand here until I'm one hundred and eighteen. It's only fair that I enjoy my pension for a couple of years before I reach one hundred and twenty. Then I'm going to travel around the world. Not to have fun, but to find out what the world smells like in the east and west, in the south and north. Then I shall die happy."

"Where have you been all this time?" Gunilla wanted to know when I got back home.

"I've been learning that people never give up."

The following morning we picked up the rental car. Needless to say they didn't give us the Volvo 40 we'd ordered and paid for, but a Nissan. I said nothing, because I've had the same conversation many times before. The company reserves the right to provide the customer with "a Volvo or a similar vehicle." This similarity refers to the engine capacity. I had protested before, insisting that I was hiring a car, not an engine, but clauses are clauses all over the world. The majestically slow assistant handed over the Nissan as if it were a Jaguar.

We drove into the center without any problems—it was impossible to drive any faster than around three miles an hour—but when we reached the main road and set off toward our destination, Gunilla noticed that the car wasn't changing gears. I pressed my foot down frantically on the gas pedal. Nothing happened. Irritated motorists sounded their horns or gave us the finger or hurled insults. I was called "a stupid old asshole," for example. The moped riders were the worst. They came right up beside me and advised me to "get a fucking move on, Granddad." Gunilla was getting more and more upset.

I used to enjoy this kind of thing once upon a time. I became energized, I fired insults back, I made the international gesture for masturbation and metamorphosed into a different person before my wife's astonished eyes.

"We have to do something," she insisted. With great difficulty I managed to find a place where I could stop for a while, and I called the car company. The majestic assistant picked up the phone, assured me that I wasn't the first customer to encounter this problem, and explained that I needed to move the stick shift from one position to another before the automatic system came into play. He informed me that this applied to all modern cars, and I could tell that he was finding it difficult not to laugh.

I shot away with a screech of tires, and asked Gunilla if we should go back and strangle the majestic assistant, which made her laugh. We decided to continue our journey without murdering anyone.

Why can't the Greeks calm down? I thought, as if I weren't a Greek myself.

Things settled down when we took the road for Elefsina, although I was always a little tense when I drove past the small town. That was where Athens ended, and we began to approach my home area of Peloponnesos, or the Peloponnese. My homeland within my homeland. Then came my village, the heart of my homeland. The cradle of all my longing, all my dreams.

My wife was absorbed in a magazine. I had spent almost a year of my military training near Elefsina, and

I remembered the endless twilights. There and on the hills all around, dusk fell more slowly than anywhere else. One day I mentioned this to my friend Little Kostas, and I have never forgotten his answer.

"Ah, Elefsina. That was where Procrustes ruled the roost. He mutilated or stretched the bodies of passing travelers in order to make them fit his iron bed. That was also where Demeter wept because her beautiful daughter was kept in the underworld. How can night fall in Elefsina?"

On all our previous trips I had told Gunilla tales of the military training facility where I almost lost my mind because of the monotony and oppression, but this time it all felt so distant. It no longer had anything to do with me. And Little Kostas was gone, the crazy boy who taught me to draw Tarzan, and the first person I ever heard talk about antimatter.

I could have said a great deal, but I said nothing.

I was a foreigner in my wife's homeland, and she was a foreigner in mine. Perhaps it was because of this mutual foreignness that we had grown so close. It felt completely natural to have her sitting beside me. So once again I said nothing.

If this was to be the last time I saw my village, I wanted Gunilla with me. She is the only one who has shared my alienation, she is the only eyewitness.

I stole a glance at her as she read, twisting her left ear as usual. I wanted to say something to her, but I kept quiet. She already knew what I wanted to say.

Some hours later we reached Epidaurus. There are few places on earth that I love as much. We clambered up to the back row of seats of the amphitheater, in spite of the fact that my wife's knee was hurting and I was as out of breath as a fish on land.

The reward was immediate. The old theater looked like an enormous flower growing in the hollow between the hills. A choir of middle-aged women were singing in Dutch and received enthusiastic applause from the other tourists. I also clapped, as if I were a tourist too. In a way I was—a tourist in a country that was once my homeland.

A group of Polish students was sitting next to us. They were exceptionally polite toward one another and everyone else, including a weary old dog that lay panting at their feet. They started talking to him and tickling him, and he livened up considerably. He lay on his back with his legs in the air, then rolled over onto his stomach and pretended to be asleep.

"What's he doing?" I asked Gunilla.

"He wants to be petted," she answered in a matter-of-fact tone of voice.

"And it works?"

"Just look at what's going on."

It worked. Why had I never thought of that? The students, particularly a blond young man called Leopold, were totally captivated by the old dog. Leopold scratched behind his ears and took pictures of him; the wretched dog was enjoying himself so much that I began to suspect he was employed by the Greek tourist board. A four-legged actor in the world's most beautiful theater.

We are no longer a country but a tourist resort. Even our animals are at the service of visitors. How did things end up this way? I shouldn't have thought about it. But I did.

I hid my sadness from my wife, who was busy taking a photograph of me.

We drove from the old Epidaurus to the new, which is by the sea. On the promenade, all the shops displayed signs in English, and the restaurants were serving pizza and Chinese food. Gunilla bought yet more postcards. The heat was beginning to get a little too much. A group of around forty people had settled down at the tables in Mike's taverna, and were engaged in a lively discussion about what they were going to eat.

"It's not a matter of life and death, boys and girls, it's just a bit of food," said a skinny man in a straw hat.

"Shut up," he was told.

They were Greek retirees taking part in the "social tourism" program. The distance between what I was looking for and what I found was growing all the time. Greece was changing without asking my permission.

The class differences were much more marked now than I remembered. The rich were richer and the poor were poorer. Great big luxury cars were parked outside the upmarket restaurant, while outside the modest taverna there were only dusty mopeds. Large private yachts were anchored in the harbor. Impressive newly built villas had appeared here and there. A short distance inland you would find scruffy little houses and tents.

It felt as if I didn't have the right to an opinion. I was a foreigner. The only thing I could say was that the country I remembered was gone.

I too had changed. I wasn't the twenty-five-year-old who went off to Sweden. I was an elderly man who had lived in Sweden for over half a century. Even if I rediscovered the Greece I remembered, I was no longer sure I would like it.

We spent the night in the old, peaceful, and very appealing town of Nafplion, which had also been a capital city in the nineteenth century. The hotel was called the Grande Bretagne, and was extremely pleasant. The staff operated in several European languages, but very little Greek was spoken. The receptionist addressed me first in German, then in French, and finally in English. There was a time when I regarded it as a compliment if someone couldn't see that I was Greek.

We went up to our magnificent suite with its antique furniture and the decorative lamps that spread a warm glow throughout the two rooms. It was late in the season, which was why we could afford it. Gunilla chose her side of the enormous double bed, which could easily have accommodated two more adults.

"It's so big we might need to speak to each other on our cell phones," she said.

Then we took a walk in the old town. It was a warm evening, and there were plenty of people out and about. Gunilla discovered an Italian *gelateria*, and what Swede can walk past one of those? The assistant spoke Italian to us, in spite of the fact that I addressed him in Greek. That gets on my nerves.

I'm not a fan of ice cream. Gunilla loves it and chose carefully from a range of different flavors with the help of two young female assistants who spoke French to her.

I sulked.

A while later we sat down in a café, and the scene from the *gelateria* was repeated. I spoke Greek to the waiter and he answered me in English. I got slightly peevish and said, "I speak a little Russian too."

"So do I," he replied in Russian.

Another surprise awaited us in the restaurant where we had decided to have dinner. We had chosen it from the outside based on one simple criterion: there was no music playing.

We were considering what to order when the waiter joined in our discussion in almost impeccable Swedish. He had worked in Sweden for several years but had left because "Greece might have all the problems in the world, but it retains life's sweetness." I asked him if I could use his words on my Twitter feed, and he had no objection.

We were treated like royalty, and this was also reflected in our check.

He wasn't wrong. Life in Greece does have a sweetness, which is difficult to define. What is it? There is an immediacy between people that can occasionally be troublesome but is mostly beneficial. There is always room around a table. A restaurant is never fully booked. A carafe of water and a basket of bread always appear before you even have time to think. The staff move like lightning, especially the pretty young women. But all this presupposes that you have money. If you don't, life becomes grim and bitter. I had lived that life, and it was the reason why I had boarded a train to Sweden. It was also the reason why I hadn't come back.

"I couldn't give a damn about life's sweetness. It's dignity I want. Without that even honey tastes bitter," I said to my wife.

Sometimes she's had enough of me.

"And what do you expect them to do?" she snapped.

I have to admit that I didn't have anything sensible to say in response. Besides, the food was sinfully delicious.

We returned to the hotel and Gunilla smoked her cigarette while we watched the city's Venetian fortress on the small island of Bourzi sink into the darkness. I was sinking into absolute alienation in roughly the same way. I wasn't even allowed to speak my language in my own country.

The following morning I awoke to an unfolding miracle. The sun was just rising, the sea mist lifted very slowly, and the mountains regained their massive splendor. It was like watching the creation of the world from the VIP seats.

I put on my wings—my Nike Air shoes—and set off along the stone pathway that curved around the hilltop above the city. I was completely alone. Suddenly I heard voices from the side on which the sea lay. I saw two fishermen, obviously old friends, because one calmly asked the other, "Shall we go to Kostas's funeral today?"

My friend Kostas had also departed, and I almost called out, "Can I come with you, boys?"

Instead I leaned on the stone balustrade pretending to rest, while in fact I was secretly watching the two fisherman in their little boat, bobbing up and down on the morning's gentle ripples like two swans wearing caps.

Nothing is more precious than a friend.

That's what Aristotle said.

Our next stop was the medieval fortress at Mystrás, built by Vilhem Villehardouin in 1249. It towers above the surrounding landscape with death-defying boldness on top of a virtually inaccessible hill. It developed into a town that became known as the Florence of the East. It was here that Plato's writings were rediscovered; they were eventually translated into Latin in Florence itself.

I wanted to show Gunilla this rare treasure, but her knee was too painful, and we had to make do with getting as far as we could by car. It was still breathtaking. From up there you could see the entire valley, the orange and lemon groves, the vineyards. The wind carried a mixture of glorious scents.

We took a short walk and soon encountered a dog, who barked rather sleepily, just for appearances' sake. Then along came his owner—a thin man around fifty years old, who immediately asked where we were from.

When he heard that we were from Sweden, he picked a few ripe figs from a sinful old tree and gave them to Gunilla.

This gesture was so familiar that for the first time during our trip I felt something awaken within me. Rule number one: You offer a stranger something—a handful of figs, a glass of water, a bunch of grapes, anything to quench his or her thirst.

It struck me that maybe the sweetness of Greek life was exactly that: a hand that gives. From one person to another. From stranger to stranger. Memories from long ago flashed through my mind. My grandmother's gnarled fingers as she pitted an olive so that I could safely eat it, my grandfather's large palm with a little yellow caramel sitting right in the middle, my mother soaking a piece of dry bread and sprinkling sugar on it.

They were cruel, hard times, but there was always a hand ready to pop something edible into a three-year-old's mouth.

Now the world was experiencing cruel, hard times once more.

Which hands would give, and which would take?

Life definitely has a sweetness in Greece, but there are elements that are nowhere near as appealing. For example, the endemic tendency to hide a fault rather than repair it. Large or small. And the constant reference to "the Greeks," which serves as an explanation for everything. Why hasn't the bus shown up? Oh, that's just the way we Greeks are. Why is the driver so unpleasant? Oh, you know what your average Greek is like. Excuse me, ladies and gentlemen, but I'm Greek too, and I'm nothing like that. In fact I hate that kind of attitude. You don't hide a hole in the floor with a rug, you *fix* it. And no, I don't know what your average Greek is like. I've never met that particular person. But I have met hundreds of wonderful people with just one fault: they say, "Oh, you know what your average Greek is like!"

Then we have the constant interrogation. Who are you? Where do you come from? What are you doing here?

It's very irritating, if you don't understand it. A stranger in Greece is not a cause for concern but a walking news desk.

It was difficult to get up to Mystrás, but the fact that we got back down was little short of a miracle. The huge tourist buses had right of way on the narrow road. I stopped every ten minutes, inches from the bottomless ravine, and let them pass.

After a while we stopped for a cup of coffee. The waitress heard us speaking a foreign language and immediately asked where we were from. Sweden. Sweden? She had a cousin there who had not only moved overseas but had sadly since emigrated to a land even farther away, the land from which no traveler returns.

What was his name? When she told me, I gave a start. He was one of my first friends in Sweden. He had died of a very aggressive cancer.

"It's strange how life makes connections," the waitress said.

Undeniably. I was sitting there with my Swedish wife, and the woman serving us was a cousin of my friend who had died in Sweden.

I felt dizzy. It was one of those moments when life stops, or is compressed into a sharp awareness of the present.

This applies to writing too. A sense of the simultaneousness of life that brings with it a controlled dizziness. I missed it terribly.

On the way to my village, we drove past another place where I had spent part of my military service. I stopped at the sentry post.

"It's forbidden to stop here," the guard said, but he calmed down when he saw my white hair.

"I've stood where you're standing," I said in a friendly tone of voice.

His words made me remember something—the time when so many things were forbidden.

It was forbidden to spit anywhere, it was forbidden to swear, it was forbidden to behave in any way that offended "public decency." The country was in a permanent state of readiness to counter a threat from the Communist countries in the north, and from Turkey.

It was a bitter time.

I had a sudden urge to turn the car around, to drive back to Athens and get on a plane to Stockholm.

But Gunilla studied the map, then looked up and said, "We have a little way to go until we reach the village."

We reached Molai shortly before three o'clock. It was an awkward time. Most people were eating, or lying down for a rest after their lunch. It suited me perfectly. I didn't arrive in my village. I entered it. It was a locked room that I had to open with a key, which had grown increasingly rusty over the years.

My heart was already pounding as we turned off the main road. I wondered where the street with my name might be, but I didn't need to wonder for very long. We came across it right away. At the sight of the sign bearing my name, I made a sound that I've never heard before. It wasn't a scream or a cry, or indeed any kind of human sound. It was like the ice breaking in early spring. It was terrifying, horrible. Fortunately it didn't last long. I scrambled up the wall as high as I could, to enable Gunilla to take a photograph of me with the sign and my street. A passing car braked sharply at the sight of an elderly madman high up on the wall, and I came to my senses.

"For this moment I wrote for all those years," I said to Gunilla.

Her eyes shone.

"I didn't even make a noise like that when I was giving birth," she said.

It might have been an exaggeration, but she knew what I liked to hear. Dear Mr. Freud focused on women's penis envy. I don't know anything about that, but I do know that my sorrow at not being able to carry a child inside my body was great. I like to regard writing as a long-drawn-out process of childbirth, even if the analogy doesn't quite work.

I also took pictures of Gunilla beneath the street sign while advising her not to post them on Facebook, because her friends would think I was dead. In Sweden we're sensible. We prefer street names such as Terapivägen—Therapy Street—or Snickarbacken—Carpenter's Hill. You have to be well and truly dead to have something named after you.

We carried on toward the square, which was more or less deserted. We took a short, hesitant walk, as if we'd never been there before. For me that was true, in a way.

I always arrive at my village for the first time.

An hour later we were at the impressive Alas Resort, where our hosts had booked a room for us. The trip from Molai to Elia, where the complex lay, usually takes less than fifteen minutes, but we couldn't find the hotel. We asked two men who were working in the simple harbor at Elia, but they knew nothing about it. They weren't local, they weren't from the next village either; in fact, they were refugees from Albania. However, they spoke excellent Greek and were very helpful. They called an acquaintance and found out the relevant information, which they passed on to us.

The hotel was on the other side of the harbor. It was visible from a distance, but not close up. We had driven past the modest sign a dozen times without spotting it.

Now we could see the hotel but no way of getting there. Eventually Gunilla discovered a secret track.

"But that leads to the sea," I said.

"In that case we'll have to swim across," she replied.

It wasn't quite that bad. Suddenly we saw an attractive building behind a magnificent bougainvillea, but there wasn't a soul in sight.

"That must be the hotel," I said, demonstrating my ability to jump to conclusions.

Once again I parked inches from the edge of a ravine and rang the bell. I could hear the sound reverberating, but no one came. We found a smaller door and rang that bell too. A short while later the door was opened by an elderly lady in a robe, with tiny red slippers on her feet. We had woken her in the middle of her siesta. She didn't seem to mind—quite the reverse. She explained how to get to the hotel in a way I will never forget.

"Keep on going until the road runs out, then carry straight on."

No sooner said than done. Ten minutes later we were there. The young woman at reception spoke perfect English, and she was good at her job. When I answered in Greek, she complimented me.

"I am Greek," I said.

"It doesn't show," she assured me.

How would it show? I wondered. Should I bear the mark of Cain on my forehead?

Our room, or rather our suite, was very pleasant. Gunilla opened all the windows and inhaled deeply, as if she wanted to take in the entire landscape, then made the comment I have been hearing for almost five decades: "There's no air in here."

The first thing she does when she walks into a hotel room is to open all the windows. She's like my mother, she wants air all the time. The second thing she does is to check whether there are enough hooks in the bathroom. She is rarely satisfied in this respect.

I called our hostess, the principal of the local high school, to let her know that we had arrived. We agreed that she would come over with some of her colleagues to say hello and to discuss the following day's event.

They were due at nine o'clock in the evening. It was closer to ten when they turned up bearing gifts, like the Danaans in the *Iliad*. Figs, grapes, chocolate, books.

Gunilla was struggling to peel a large, beautiful fig with a knife and fork when the principal, who was also the director of the next day's theatrical performance, pointed out that it would be easier to use her hands. Gunilla obeyed like a schoolgirl.

It was lovely to see that they were trying to make sure she didn't feel like an outsider. She was given the opportunity to speak English, French, and German, although by the time we all said good night, much, much later, she was able to say "*efkaristo poli*," which means "thank you very much."

Many people have wondered over the years why Gunilla didn't make more of an effort to learn Greek, and why I didn't try to persuade her to do so, or why I didn't speak Greek with my children.

The main reason is simple: the need for me to constantly improve my Swedish. I was a writer, I loved my new language, and I exploited both my wife and children in order to become more fluent. On top of this, Gunilla is very rigid about her language, and as she has grown older she has become a real martinet when it comes to both grammar and pronunciation. "It's not *schafför*," she says with distaste, pulling a face in front of the TV.

The children also taught me words like *möka* (to fart) or *fetto* (fat) and *svullo* (greedy guts). We had long discussions about the correct way to conjugate *möka*. Should it be *möka*, *mök*, or *möka*, *mökte*, or perhaps *möka*, *mökade*?

Who else could teach me those words?

My defense is that simple. I plead guilty, with great pleasure and joy.

We sat on the balcony for a while, listening to the sea and looking at the lights around the inlet. Gunilla smoked her cigarette.

"Did you have a good time?" I asked her.

"I've never tasted better figs and grapes."

"I meant the people."

She thought for a moment.

"If all Greeks were like them, Greece wouldn't have any problems," she answered eventually.

The next day we met up with two friends, Danae and Giannis. They were the only ones I remembered from my childhood; they knew my parents and siblings. To visit them without being offered food is unthinkable. We had a wonderful lunch and talked about the forthcoming performance.

Giannis owned Aeschylus's collected tragedies, neatly arranged in alphabetical order in his cool, muted study.

For a brief moment I envied them their life. The house was one of the oldest in the village, with large rooms, high ceilings, handmade antique furniture. The terrace was filled with the scent of basil. I remembered Danae as a young woman—she was the great beauty of the village—tending her plants with a silver watering can every afternoon, hovering eighteen inches above the ground.

I also wanted to visit Aunt Argiro, who was the last member of our family still living in the village. So we took our leave of Danae, who naturally gave us a homemade plum-and-raisin cake approximately the size of a small pig.

Giannis went with us to show us the way. My aunt still lives in the house that once belonged to my maternal grandparents. Her husband was my beloved uncle, and he inherited the small property and expanded it. My aunt continued after his death, and eventually it became an extensive three-story building. It turned out that Aunt Argiro was still busy with improvements, in spite of her age and the fact that she could no longer see very well. However, she was as lively as a little girl, quick to smile and laugh. She opened her arms wide when she saw us, her coal-black eyes sparkling with happiness.

"How are you, my child?" she asked Gunilla in dazzling Greek.

"*Kala, poli kala,*" Gunilla replied. Good, very good.

"You speak Greek well, my daughter!" my aunt rejoiced. She was also very taken with my wife's appearance and pretended to spit three times to keep away the evil eye.

My reception, however, was significantly more critical.

"You are too thin, my precious," she said. "You must eat!"

She was eager to prepare a light meal, but we refused with determination and settled for going out onto the terrace to watch the sun setting slowly over the valley. The shadows grew longer and longer until the sun disappeared behind the high mountains in the distance, leaving only a shimmer of pink and blue.

I thought about the battle of Molai between the resistance fighters and the Germans, although I didn't understand its significance back then. I was just over five years old in December 1943. I saw men edging slowly toward the village, stopping from time to time to fire off a salvo.

That was all I remembered. Everything else had disappeared. I remembered my maternal grandparents, but these sparse memories seemed to belong to someone else. It wasn't me standing on this terrace, but what was left of me.

My aunt was a lovely old tree, aging as it grew.

The emigration that had begun seventy years ago when I left my village to move to Athens, and continued when I arrived in Sweden, was still going on. This time I was emigrating from myself. I was gradually becoming someone else.

I didn't count before I left Greece. I was no one, but I was me. The family philosopher, my mother's son, the local football team's outside left, the pupil who wrote the best essays. All this was lost in the wind, or on a train heading for somewhere else.

Who or what would restore me to myself?

I looked around over and over again, hoping that something would awaken within me, some aspect of all those things I remembered, but it felt as if I were watching a grainy old film. My memories had lost their strength. That was why it was no longer possible to write. I was empty inside, like an old walnut. It looked whole and healthy, but the flesh within had shriveled until it had no nutritional value.

We didn't stay long with Aunt Argiro and she didn't get the opportunity to feed us, but she made sure she seized the chance to remind me once again that I was too thin. To be on the safe side, she also told my wife that she must make sure that I ate a little more.

We returned to the hotel at about six o'clock. Gunilla felt the need to go down to the sea and wanted to swim. We walked along the shore, and I watched as she entered the water at a leisurely pace and began to swim, without dipping her head beneath the waves. I have never seen her emerge from the water with wet hair. I went in to keep her company, but I dipped my head over and over again in the hope of waking from my lethargy.

It didn't work.

It was September 26, the night of the supermoon, if you remember that. The performance was due to begin in the village's small amphitheater at eight thirty. It was already busy when we got there, and more people were arriving all the time.

I felt as if I were witnessing a requiem mass dedicated to me. The moon up in the sky kept on growing.

The mayor gave a speech, as did the cultural representative for the area. Finally our hostess spoke—the director of the performance and the school principal, Olympia Lampoussi.

I saw them, I heard them, they were wonderful people, but what was it they were talking about? Was it me? Was I dreaming while still awake?

Then the lights went out, except on the stage and in the sky. A drum in the background provided the rhythm for the teenagers who appeared dressed in the silvery darkness of the star-studded night, their costumes glowing faintly and making them look both ceremonial and ethereal.

This was the chorus. I got goose bumps as soon as they uttered the opening words.

While o'er the fields of Greece the embattled troops
Of Persia march with delegated sway,
We o'er their rich and gold-abounding seats
Hold faithful our firm guard...

So Aeschylus began, speaking directly to us. We were not an audience; we were a part of the play.

The young actors knew what they were talking about. I have seen famous people playing classical tragedy and failing to connect with either the words or the audience. But these young voices could do it. I gave myself up to them, to the words of Aeschylus, and my heart almost burst with pride.

Was there anywhere else in the world where high school students performed Aeschylus? Was there?

The moon was now so huge and so close that it looked as if it were holding on to the sky with its teeth. Then all of a sudden there was a power outage.

Who switched off the moon? This absurd question came into my mind.

There was a brief pause, the power came back on, the play continued. That's exactly what used to happen in my childhood. The power came and went all night long. Life paused, then continued after a few minutes.

That was how it felt on this occasion too, as if life were starting again from the beginning. Aeschylus's words fell like cooling rain on parched earth.

This language was my language.

I was perspiring heavily, with large beads of sweat shining on my forehead, and Gunilla whispered in my ear, "Take off your jacket."

"There's no need. It's cool in Greek."

The performance was a triumph. The audience applauded loudly and for a long time, particularly because it was made up of the parents and relatives of those involved. I don't say this with the intention of devaluing their enthusiasm; the performance was quite simply very, very good.

I had to make a short speech of thanks, but I was so moved, my legs were shaking. I stumbled and was in danger of making a rather more spectacular entrance than I would have wished, but one of the teachers took me by the arm, and eventually I was standing on the stage in front of everyone like a shipwrecked sailor, finding it difficult to breathe. I knew that Gunilla was on her feet like the rest of the audience, I looked for her but couldn't find her, the young actors surrounded me with glowing, bottomless eyes that I will never forget, they had brought copies of my books for me to sign, I exchanged a few words with each one of them.

The evening was further enhanced by the dinner that took place beneath the open sky, with the usual cascade of small dishes.

I was seated a short distance away from Gunilla, and I glanced at her from time to time to see if she was enjoying herself. It was better than that. She was having the time of her life. The young fair-haired English teacher who had visited our hotel room was there to help once more, which reassured me.

We sat there until long after midnight. A very kind married couple who were both physicians drove us back to our hotel. The husband had the same problem as me, with the same result. He was trying to give up smoking. Without success.

The following morning I was up early and was sur-
prised by a storm. The wind was blowing, the sea
was rough. Dark clouds in the sky. Then came a down-
pour, almost passionate in its intensity.

The weather wasn't going to affect my plans. I
went down to the hotel restaurant where guests could
make themselves a cup of instant coffee. I sat down at
a table. My pulse rate must have been somewhere in
the region of one eighty, my heart was pounding like a
jackhammer.

I opened the computer, changed the language from
Swedish to Greek, and waited for the first word. The
waves were getting higher and higher, and the rain
was rattling against the windowpane. I waited. Nothing happened. I tried to think in Greek, but that didn't
help. Swedish was the language in which I had written
all my books.

I switched back to Swedish, but nothing was going
on in my brain. I had gathered so many impressions
during this trip, made so many notes, but everything felt
lifeless, stone dead.

I sat there for almost an hour without writing a single word. I was caught between my two languages like

Buridan's famous donkey, who died of both hunger and thirst because it couldn't decide whether to eat or drink.

I hadn't said anything to Gunilla. She was unaware of my plans to write in Greek. I didn't want to tell anyone. I feared the self-evident objections. How could I possibly write in a language I hadn't used in a literary context since the age of twenty?

I had heard all this when I started writing in Swedish. How could I possibly write in a language that wasn't mine? But I did.

I went back to Greek and waited. Gunilla came down a while later, we had breakfast together. The weather had dampened her spirits a little, but she took a practical view of the rain.

"I'm sure it's needed," she said, and wanted to know what I was doing on the computer at such an early hour.

"I was playing chess."

She knew I was lying but said nothing. Instead she took out a pile of the postcards she'd bought and started writing, as if it were the easiest thing in the world.

For heaven's sake, I'm going to do the same thing! I thought. I opened the computer once more, thought about a dear friend in Sweden, and set to work.

It was a difficult time. After the very first word I was aware of an incomprehensible sweetness in my mouth, as if I had eaten honey. Sweetness and relief.

I wasn't writing. I was speaking. One word joined the next like small siblings. I wasn't afraid of making mistakes, even though I knew I would. This was my language. It didn't impose itself upon me, it wasn't necessary to change my tone of voice.

In Swedish, which I loved and will always love, I had never reached this immediacy, this sense of restfulness. I probably never would. The language was a crown of thorns upon my head, not a heartbeat. The result was neither better nor worse, it was simply different. Would it be possible to marry my two languages together?

I rewrote the first sentence in Swedish, trying to be completely faithful to the original Greek.

It couldn't be done. In order to be anywhere near good in Swedish, it had to be changed. Not completely and not too much, but the world of one language was different from the other. So was the rhythm. And the idea of time, the sense of timing. But mainly the rhythm. Swedish flowed along one inlet, Greek along another.

The conclusion is simple. Each language is unique. You can't write the same book in two different languages. You write a book that resembles the one you've already written.

That's all.

You can say what is to be said in every language in the world.

You can also say nothing about it.

Or talk about something else.

The latter is best done in your mother tongue.

The following day we went home to Sweden, but this time I was not an immigrant. I thought about the migrating bird flying all alone across the Gotland sky; it had lost its flock but not the direction in which it had to travel. The reverse was true of me. I hadn't lost my flock, but I had lost the direction.

It was restored to me by the words of Aeschylus, by those boys and girls and their teacher, Olympia Lampoussi.

This short book—the first I have written in Greek in more than fifty years—is my belated thanks to them for taking me back to my language, the only homeland I had, and one that would never let me down.

Not only did they show me an almost unbearable appreciation, which became my salvation, they also saved that which could be saved.

So what did it matter where in the world I would spend my life?

Huddinge, February 28, 2016
Theodor Kallifatides

THEODOR KALLIFATIDES has published more than forty works of fiction, nonfiction, and poetry that have been translated around the world. Born in Greece in 1938, Kallifatides immigrated in 1964 to Sweden, where he began his literary career. As a translator, he has brought August Strindberg and Ingmar Bergman to Greek readers, and Giannis Ritsos and Mikis Theodorakis to Swedish ones. He has received numerous awards for his work in both Greece and Sweden. He lives in Sweden.

MARLAINE DELARGY is best known for her translations of the work of Henning Mankell, John Ajvide Lindqvist, and Kristina Ohlsson. She is also the translator of Therese Bohman's *Eventide*, *The Other Woman*, and *Drowned* (Other Press). She serves on the editorial board of the *Swedish Book Review*. She lives in Shropshire, England.

◨ OTHER PRESS

You might also enjoy these titles from our list:

HOW TO LIVE: A LIFE OF MONTAIGNE
by Sarah Bakewell
WINNER OF THE 2010 NATIONAL BOOK CRITICS CIRCLE
AWARD FOR BIOGRAPHY

A spirited and singular biography of Michel de
Montaigne by way of the questions he posed and
the answers he explored

"A biography in the form of a delightful conversation
across the centuries." —*New York Times*

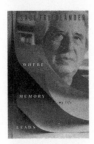

WHERE MEMORY LEADS by Saul Friedländer

A Pulitzer Prize–winning historian's return to memoir,
a tale of intellectual coming-of-age on three continents

"A gripping, troubling narrative... Page after page we
feel we are getting closer to [Friedländer]. Then we
suddenly realize how inscrutable an individual life
is — to us, to the narrator himself." —Carlo Ginzburg

WHAT YOU DID NOT TELL: A FATHER'S PAST
AND THE JOURNEY HOME by Mark Mazower
SHORTLISTED FOR THE 2018 ORWELL PRIZE

A warm, insightful memoir by an acclaimed historian
that explores the struggles of twentieth-century Europe
through the lives and hopes of a single family — his own

"*What You Did Not Tell* is, in the end, a profound
testament to the saving grace of a sense of rootedness
in place and home." —*New York Times Book Review*